Donated by
Joseph and Diane Bast
to The Heartland Institute
2015

HUMAN HISTORY

viewed as

SOVEREIGN INDIVIDUALS

versus

MANIPULATED MASSES

from the
Valorian Society

Published by
SOVEREIGN PRESS
326 Harris Road
Rochester, WA 98579

Copyright © Valorian Society 1986
All rights reserved – no part of this book
may be reproduced in any form without permission
in writing from the copyright owner.

Manufactured in the United States of America

ISBN 0-914752-23-5

Library of Congress Catalog Card Number 86-60241

CONTENTS

THE BASIC LANGUAGE: REALITY	7
THE USE AND MISUSE OF WORDS	13
HUMAN CULTURE OF HUMANS	15
TWO CULTURES OPPOSING EVOLUTION	17
ONE CULTURE OPPOSING THE OTHER TWO	23
OPPOSING CULTURES CANNOT BE MIXED	27
AN ATTRACTIVE FRONT FOR MASS MANIPULATION	29
CONFLICT BETWEEN CULTURES	34
THE MAKING OF A GROUP-ENTITY	40
A GROUP-ENTITY WITHOUT ADORNMENT	43
SOME ATTEMPTS TO MIX CULTURES	47
WORDS USED TO COMMUNICATE AND WORDS AS WEAPONS OF DESTRUCTION	51
A COMBINATION OF MISUSED WORDS AND FORCE	58
MONEY	63
THE REVOLT OF THE VIKINGS	67
SEGREGATION PROVIDES A NEW OPPORTUNITY	70
THE CURRENT WORLDWIDE PICTURE	79
ABOUT THE BOOK'S AUTHORS	89

THE BASIC LANGUAGE: REALITY

We humans usually recognize something we call reality that is different from our thoughts and dreams. It includes matter that has continuity in time, extension in space, and a force, or will, that overrides our thoughts and dreams. Most of us divide matter into two categories: non-living matter and living things.

We, and all living things, have command over the force of a limited portion of matter that we call our bodies. Our will uses the force of this limited portion of matter to interact with the world of reality.

All living things eat, or absorb matter that is not part of their bodies, and thereby increase the portion of matter that responds to their wills.

Some humans have become fascinated by their ability to manipulate the force in non-living matter. The fascination that some find in manipulating what is outside themselves, living things as well as non-living matter, goes to an extreme that triggers opposition from others.

The total amount of matter that has extension in space and continuity in time is awesomely great in comparison to that which is under the command of an individual's will. We can postulate that there is, or was, a will controlling the whole; or we can postulate that the force in non-living matter is not, and possibly has never been, under the command of a will similar to our own.

The authors of this work recognize that we, we living things, have creative consciousness. Our current knowledge indicates that we evolved from an aboriginal single cell. Because our creative consciousness is born as part of us, we think it is sound reasoning to assume that there is, or was, an aboriginal creative consciousness from which our own was born – and to assume that creative consciousness of the same heritage, along with the will that directs the force of our bodies, is within all living things.

Some humans try to communicate their impressions of total reality to other humans in words. The invention and use of words might be a great accomplishment if words were used exclusively to communicate. However, a misuse of words - the use of words, not to communicate but to control the will of others - has created a worldwide problem for the human species.

Mass warfare is a very conspicuous aspect of this problem.

A less conspicuous aspect is peaceful mass acquiesence to the acts of those who are poisoning the earth, air, and water on which all living things depend.

A third, but still less conspicuous aspect, is the destruction of human life's quality by the use of manipulated masses to destroy individual freedom. The manipulated masses force individuals to surrender their innate sovereignty and creative consciousness to a fictional sovereignty and will that is claimed as a group prerogative by the groups' manipulators.

Word-controlled groups are crowding out all direct interaction between individuals and total reality. Human individuals are ceasing to function as anything other than parts of a group. The quality of individual human life is being reduced to that of a cell in a multicelled organism.

This work will examine the specific misuse of words that has led to this condition. Its authors view the trend as undesirable and want to reverse it. This work presents that viewpoint for open discussion.

Reversing the present trend means consciously rejecting the misuse of words for mass manipulation and reclaiming our individual sovereignty from the word manipulated group. This cannot be done by creating a new word manipulated group. It can only be done by the cooperative effort of conscious, perceptive, reasoning individuals. Our examination of the workings of a non-manipulated group of perceptive individuals will give us an example that was once a major world force.

Words, which override the perception and will inherited from the aboriginal creative consciousness, are imposed on most children while they are extremely young. Overriding the newborn individual's innate consciousn perception with words may be done willfully, or may be done unintentionally because inprecisions and double meanings are built into the language.

We will try to avoid confusing words, and limit what we postulate about the currently functioning long range direction of the creative consciousness to what can be deduced by observing the world of reality.

* * *

Our individual creative consciousness operates in the universe of time.

We observe that we evolved from single cells through a process of evolution. The process of evolution operates in the universe of time and its observable direction exists in the universe of time.

Without discussing time, space, and non-living matter, we are beginning this history with the first living things, from which it is generally assumed that we have unbroken continuity. If we respect ourselves we must respect something - a value, creative consciousness, force, will, or whatever we name it - that is identified with the process of evolution. If that something were not operative, we would still be egg-heads without bodies, little balls, single cells floating in the soup with other single cells.

We will orient on what our observation of the evolutionary process tells us about the long range direction of that something - which we call the aboriginal creative consciousness - during the time that the creative function can be seen in living things.

From the facts that can be observed, we assume that the first single cell grew and then divided itself and became two.

This cell division is the first observable indication of the direction established by the process of evolution. Each of the two new cells that came from the first divided in the same way. This happened again and again.

Then some of the cells began to stay together and cooperate. In time they began to specialize. Some took in the food. Some passed it around to the others. Some threw out what was left that none of them wanted.

This specialization went on until the cells within the cooperative organization could not survive alone. When we see that happen, we begin to think of the total group of specialized, cooperating cells as the living thing. We call the thing we are focusing our attention on and talking about an entity. When the cells cannot survive alone, we change our focus and think about the multi-celled thing as the new living entity.

Some living entities take most of their food from the earth and sunlight. Some get their food by eating the others. Eating instead of being eaten became an early basis of the evolutionary process that selected living entities for survival. When finding good things to eat and eating them was the only relationship between living things they all seemed to have enjoyed it. It appears that this went on for over two thousand million years.

Then, maybe about six hundred million years ago, the evolutionary process resulted in a new pattern that we call sex. Before sex each living entity merely divided itself to make a new entity. Sex, as a condition for species survival, requires that two different entities come together, that each give part of itself, and the parts be joined to make a new entity.

Sex introduced a new way of selecting living things for evolutionary survival. Species survival required a sexual creature to enjoy perception of another living entity without eating and making it part of itself.

The old evolutionary pattern of eat or be eaten was still part of the evolutionary selective process. Sex did not replace it. Sex was added to it. In order to continue as part of the time flowing direction of evolution, living entities of the new kind had to work both into their pattern of living.

Survival on the evolutionary plateau of sex required improved perception. The evolutionary process selected for survival those who could perceive and find value in an entity other than oneself. We have observed that enjoyment of living is part of the inborn force, or will, that characterizes living things. On the sexual plateau, perceptive enjoyment of an entity different from oneself as an objective whole – rather than as something to be torn up and made part of oneself – became part of the evolutionary pattern that selected living entities for survival.

The attempts of various species to work out the best pattern for sexual relations provide numerous models that we can see, think about, and use as examples to consider when making conscious choices regarding what might be best for ourselves.

Some worms have male and female parts all lined up in one living entity. Some shell fish change sex from male to female and back again depending on what mates are available. Among some fish the male is so much smaller than the female that it is difficult to recognize that they are the same species. Among some insects the female, after the male gives her the parts of himself to make a new entity, goes back to the more primitive stage of evolution and eats the male.

Among most animals that are enough like humans for us to feel companionable with them, the male is usually bigger than the female because he fights off intruders while the female takes care of the young. Also he fights other males who want to mate with the same female that he does. The innate sexual difference in behavior among dogs and horses is often conspicuous enough to be impressive. We see it as a sexual division that affects evolution by balancing (1) creation by selective destruction with (2) creation by cherishing and preserving. This sexual division forms complimentary, perception-stimulating perspectives – balanced by being divided between two individuals – that can be effectively used by conscious creative humans. We, therefore, view it in ourselves as a desirable trait that we want to preserve.

A method of dealing with sex that can be seen as a serious warning when considering possible human choices is what the so-called "social" insects – the ants, termites, and some species of bees – did to their sexual beings. They would be more accurately called the "regressive" insects. After they had become sexual entities they turned their own evolutionary development backward. They returned to the state of evolution that existed before sexual perception became a factor of evolutionary selection. The individuals that were once sexual beings lost their sex and took on the function of specialized cells in the overall new entity they developed – the ant or termite hill or the bee hive.

This example is important to us because humans are now doing the same thing. Humans are specializing and destroying their inborn sexual behavior. They are forming group-entities made up of living components who are no longer allowed to behave as separate individuals.

Most animals have a much sharper sense of smell than humans. Odors are as important to them as words are to humans. To them, sex odors are extremely strong, and extremely persuasive. Most animals use sex odors to find mates and then make perceptive selection among the mates they find.

The "social" insects misused sex odors to turn their evolutionary development backwards and create new group-entities that were asexual. They rejected the discriminating sexual perception bred into individuals and went back to where all living things were six hundred million years ago.

Humans are now using words to do the same thing that these regressive insects did with sex odors. We, who do not like that direction, want to look at how words can be used to communicate and how they have been, and are being, misused to manipulate masses and create group-entities that function as asexual organisms.

THE USE AND MISUSE OF WORDS

As soon as humans began to use words, parents could tell their children about things the children hadn't seen, and tell the children what foods were good to eat, where to get them, how to build fires, how to cook, how to build houses to keep out the rain and snow. As long as words were used as pointers to reality, they did not stop the children from thinking for themselves. Words stimulated thinking.

The problem that humans have created for themselves results from the way words are used in combination with force. Words alone are not the problem. And force alone is not the problem.

The ability of a living thing to use the force of its body is what lets us know that it a living thing. The use of this force to oppose other living things is part of the process of evolution.

If we wanted to break up the combination that causes the problem we should choose to do away with the use of words rather than the use of force. Words are a very recent experiment as compared to three billion years that force has been used. We must recognize that force is here to stay.

All animals use force to get others to do or not do what they want or don't want. The use of force is the way the mother horse or mother dog gets the young horse or young dog to do or not do what the mother wants or doesn't want. The use of force is the way human parents get children to do or not do what they want or don't want before the children have learned about words. Force is what adult animals, including adult humans, use in their relations to other adults who oppose what they want to do.

Among non-human adult animals, and among human adults, opposing wills often lead to fights and one of two contestants gets killed. When the process of evolution is operating in its natural way, and when the fight goes to the death of one contestant, the process breeds out the weak and stupid. It breeds out the weak in favor of the strong. It breeds out the stupid who lack the perception to know that they should run, make friends, or otherwise avoid getting into the fight in the first place.

Forcing one's will upon another does not go against the process of evolution. Also, using words to convince another to do what one wants done does not go against the process of evolution.

However, humans have misused a combination of force and words to oppose natural evolution.

HUMAN CULTURE OF HUMANS

We use the word "culture" to mean the selection of living things that is done by humans, instead of by the process of natural evolution. Corn culture is planting seeds of corn, making conditions favorable for their growth, and killing off other living things that interfere with that growth. Culture is the use of human will and force to select what will live and what will die. Culture can go the same direction as natural evolution or oppose it.

Human culture of humans is a process that uses words and force in a combination that selects the kind of humans who will survive and become part of the stream of evolution. It may select in a way that merely speeds up natural evolution or it may select in a way that goes opposite to the long-range direction indicated by evolution.

Natural evolution, which can be traced from the first living cell to humans, makes for the awesome variety of living things that oppose each other in the struggle for survival. The process that selects for survival goes in an observable direction. The creative interaction between individual wills, and between the will, or force, that overrides all individual wills, is the overall selective process to which we all owe our very existence. If we perceive and respect our existence within the universe of reality, we cannot fail to perceive and respect the efficacy of the evolutionary process. Respect for its demonstrated efficacy stimulates awe for that not-clearly-perceived something that results in the observable long range direction of evolution.

However, at the present time the entire world is dominated by two cultures that both oppose natural evolution. Both would ultimately take the human species back to where all living things were six hundred million years ago. There is immediate danger that they will take us past the point of no return. Avoiding this danger calls for an examination of how words and force have been, and are being, combined to override innate perception.

The words used by these two cultures may be based on a sincere conviction that humans should oppose the process of evolution and should try to achieve "victory over nature." Or they may be based on simple selfishness that is not concerned with the overall reality. Or they may be the deliberate lies of those seeking to manipulate others because the feeling of "power over others" satisfies some psychotic impulse.

The force used by these two cultures may involve bare hands, beating sticks, swords, guns, atomic bombs, confinement in jails, torture, or anything else.

These cultures, created by the combination of force and words and opposing the long-range direction set by Nature, are what concern us.

Both of these cultures were fully active at the time the first story of humans was set down in words. We are going to look at both of them.

Also, we are going to look at another culture – one that went in the same direction as natural evolution. This other culture was caught in a squeeze between the two that go against evolution. It is now no longer actively functioning. Unless it can be re-established, the human species will doubtless either create permanent, "successful" group-entities and, like the "social" insects, go all the way back to the eat or be eaten condition that existed before sex – or destroy itself.

Both of the dominating cultures are essentially the same in that they oppose Nature. But, because their patterns of combining force and words are slightly different, we will look at them separately. Because we are looking mostly at their words as tools of manipulation, we can only talk about human cultures of humans when we know about their words. At the time we have the first knowledge of them in words, one of these Nature-opposing cultures dominated the Orient, and still does. The other dominated the Mediterranean area and now dominates the whole Western World.

TWO CULTURES OPPOSING EVOLUTION

ORIENTAL

A human culture of humans is based on some combination of force and words. In the Orient force was used to back up the word-expressed idea that, even when a human became an adult, he should let another think and make decisions for him. Of course, that was not presented as a fundamental idea and adopted because it appealed to native perception. The combination of force and words was built up gradually. It began by keeping the family together until the grandparents told the young parents and the children of the young parents what to do. It was not force but a word-imposed concept of "obligation" that fashioned the initial word-implement used in the culture.

As families grew to hundreds, to thousands, there was less individual perception of individuals. The "obligatory" behavior patterns for children, for young adults, for young parents, and for the older decision makers became formalized. The move toward a culture began when parents chose mates for their children on the basis of conformity to formalized behavior. Those whose perception was strong enough to make them intractable to the practice had no children and were bred out of the species.

Individual perception of total reality was crowded out by the pressure on each newborn child to learn the specifically human social behavior that was accepted by all around. Then, as the child grew, perception of total reality was further crowded out by pressure to become proficient in conformity to what was accepted specifically by "social" humans. Individual humans did not relate to total reality directly. They related to total reality only as it affected their human group as a whole.

Also they did not relate to other individual humans directly. They related to other individual humans as seen through a "social" behavior pattern that had been made to appear more important than innate perception.

Perception bred by sexual being, and the resultant overall increase in perception when viewing ones relation to total reality and to other individuals, was being bred out by pressure for social conformity.

As families grew into great groups, group fought group for living room. Survival became a simple matter of being in the biggest group or the one with the best fighters.

The premise of the Oriental culture that ultimately overruled perception was that group power is a condition of human existence. It was followed by the corollary that intelligent people will accept that condition as an immutable fact and concentrate on how best to improve the prescribed behavior and defend the group one is in against other groups.

The word-expressed idea that was combined with force to form the human culture of humans in the Orient was very simple. It was nothing but this: "Everyone must recognize that an individual cannot fight a big group and therefore must accept someone as controlling the group he happens to be in, making his significant decisions for him, and telling him what to do." The non-conformists were bred out either by killing them for "anti-social" behavior or by not allowing them to have children.

The people talked about and respected the memory of their ancestors and invented some of the imaginary beings that are called gods, which they often thought were real. However the ancestor worship, and the rituals involving the idea of gods, were no more than decorations added to their culture.

The Oriental culture of humans, that opposed natural evolution, was based on simple recognition that a group is more powerful than an individual.

That simple fact, which could not be disputed, was made into a force-backed social pressure that prevented socially acceptable discussion that might examine related facts. Anyone who might ask, "Why create group power in the first place?" would be shunned as stupid.

Such force-backed social pressure left one who did not like the group he was in no option but to create a bigger and more powerful group. And creating a bigger and more powerful group required appealing to the practice of group-entities dominating individuals, which already was the only idea widely accepted. Full acceptance of the idea therefore had to be the basis for any new group formation.

At the time of our first word histories of the Orient, human culture of humans had already crowded out natural evolution - and turned the direction set by natural evolution backward.

WESTERN

The human culture of humans that first became dominant in the Mediterranean area, and now dominates the whole Western World, selectively breeds for group-entities in the same way as that in the Orient. But the words used in combination with group force are more complicated. The big group, that is too formidable for an individual to fight, does not come about simply because the children stay together and continue to let the words of the parents overrule their own thoughts after they are adults.

When we look at the first record of the Western people in words, they had already invented imaginary beings that they called gods. These imaginary gods, unlike the gods of the Orient, were a very important part of the culture that went against the process of evolution. Each group had its own god, the god was said to give orders to special individuals who then told the others what to do. When a god-spokesman had a sufficient number of followers to overpower dissenters, the manipulated followers killed those in the group who would not obey the god-spokesman.

The emphasis was not simply on demanding that everyone comform to the will of the group's manipulators. The emphasis was on the demand that words - which were supposed to have come from a god - replace thought. The god was said to be someone whose words had to be obeyed without understanding.

When we look at the first record of Western group-entity formation, there were already many different group-entities and numerous gods. The groups fought each other. The people in a group that was overpowered were forced to throw out their old god and accept the words supposed to have come from another god.

None of these gods even remotely resembled what might be deduced about the aboriginal creative consciousness by observing reality. These were all man-invented gods, all different but all diametrically opposed to the direction manifest by the aboriginal creative consciousness.

The god-oriented culture of mass manipulation that came to dominate the West, unlike the similar Oriental culture that began by adults continuing to obey their parents and grandparents, conditioned people to obey a source for "authoritative" words that was intangible, a source that could not be clearly identified and confronted.

This conditioning to accept a purported source of will that cannot be confronted has continued. It is the special form of brainwashing now most commonly used by manipulators in the West. Western manipulators, who capitalize on this extant brainwashing, have inserted a new intangible and unidentifiable source called "the consensus of the best scientific opinion" to override individual perception. They are trying to use it as a replacement for the gods that were originally accepted as speaking "authoritative" words.

Like the "authority" purportedly coming from gods, what the current manipulators have chosen as "the consensus of the best scientific opinion" becomes part of the characteristic Western culture of mass manipulation. Like the "god authority," this abitrarily chosen "scientific authority" cannot be clearly identified and confronted. And, like the "god authority," it opposes Nature, and what might be learned about the aboriginal creative consciousness by observing the direction the evolution of living things has taken.

The newly invented "god," the "consensus of the best scientific opinion," which is the extremely unscientific opinion that the manipulators select to support their will, claims: (1) That mutations are accidents, (2) that sex is merely another accidentally developed method of reproduction, (3) that living things, themselves, are merely an accidental development of brainless matter, and (4) that there is no such thing as an aboriginal creative consciousnes as the progenitor of human creative consciousness.

After presenting such untenable statements as "scientific facts," the manipulators claim that "the consensus of the best scientific opinion" should replace the old gods as the new source of "authoritative" words. We will discuss the spokesmen for this newly invented "god" later.

Even before this new ambiguity was injected into the field of man-invented gods, it all became so confusing that the word "government" for the humans "authorized" to give orders in the group-entity was often used instead of talking about which god was the source of the force-backed "authority."

We might describe a government as the formal implement of a people's culture. But we think that any fruitful analysis of the human problem will require us to keep our focus on the cultures, themselves.

The significant thing about the separate cultures that arose in Orient and the Western World is this: Although the words and ideas are different, the evolution-opposing selective effect of both is the same. Both promote the idea that it is impossible for an individual to live outside a group controlled by mass manipulators. All the governments that implement these two cultures use group force to back the idea that everybody must become part of some group, must accept some source of "authority" as controlling the group, doing the thinking for every individual, and telling everyone what to do.

EVOLUTION TURNED BACKWARDS

The selective breeding that results from both of these two human cultures of humans goes in same regressive direction long ago taken by the "social" insects.

These two human cultures of humans have now crowded out all effective opposition to the direction they are going.

More than that, they have tried to wipe out the record that there ever was any effective cultural opposition to their direction.

Because they now dominate the entire world, they have almost reached their goal of wiping out, or twisting into unrecognizable form, the knowledge that such opposition once successfully existed.

They have already competely erased the record of the opposing culture from all history books provided for compulsory "education."

If they can wipe out the memory completely, they may be able to force on everyone the brainwashing which claims that there is no alternative to mass manipulation. Then the human species will have passed the point of no return.

But as of now we still have a record of such opposition and we know how it was made ineffective. The only hope that the human species will not go the way of the regressive insects requires reviving the culture that goes the same direction as natural evolution. So we need to think about such a culture and look at the one known example.

ONE CULTURE OPPOSING THE OTHER TWO

The early people of Western Asia and Northern Europe provide the one historically known example of a human culture of humans selecting in the same direction as natural evolution. Apparently aware of what was happening on both sides of them, they had consciously created a culture of their own in opposition to what others were doing. It was unique.

In an attempt to distract attention from this unique culture, the mass manipulators lump the people who had developed it into the same category with the primitives of their own cultures and categorize them all by the derogatory term "barbarians."

The mass manipulators do not want it recognized that their own human culture of humans produces the problem facing the human species. They try to avoid discussing human culture of humans and the conflict between cultures. They refer to the destruction of the individual sovereignty culture of Northern Europe as "civilizing the barbarians."

In Europe, the Catholic Church pushed that interpretation of "civilizing the barbarians" to account for its several hundred years of torture, inquisitions, and public executions of all individuals who opposed mass manipulation. The mass manipulators who now control television and movies in the United States, and for fifty years have dominated the school system, have pushed that viewpoint to such an extent that some points in support of what will follow need to be offered for the reader's consideration.

Some of the earliest examples of fine workmanship are the artifacts found in Europe. This, coupled with the Northern European mythology that those of noble character have disdain for the kind of "wealth" that gives status in "civilizations," indicates that the people knew as much as others about manufacturing, but had come to place a higher value on things of the natural world.

The remains of some of the earliest mines for extracting minerals are found in Europe. These give evidence that the kind of "civilization" that requires either slaves, or the mass manipulation of menial laborers, had been tried and then abandoned. It did not exist in Northern Europe at the time of the first word records.

The extant early word records on which we must depend are those of Julius Caesar, written in the first century B. C., and Tacitus, written in the first century A. D. The mass manipulators try to discredit the praise Tacitus gave to the people of Germania for having a better way of life than the people of the Roman Empire. They try to imply that he might have had the bias of a utopian reformer. But certainly Caesar, who was describing an enemy he was trying to conquer, cannot be accused of falsifying in the enemy's favor. The accounts of both Tacitus and Caesar support what we are about to describe.

Also, the remembered desire for "individualism," that was still strong among the descendants of the Northern Europeans who formed the United States, bears evidence of a long existing culture other than mass manipulation. After a thousand years under the Catholic Church's intense pressure on the people to abandon their traditional values as "evil," the people who formed the United States set forth a Declaration of Independence and a Constitution in support of individual sovereignty. Even the practice of one-to-one dueling remained legal in many states until the Civil War and was still practiced after that by rough and ready cowboys in territories that had not become states.

If, even after considering these points, some readers still adhere to the "barbarian" brand, which the mass manipulators place on the Northern Europeans who rejected manipulation, they are invited to consider the following as the kind of culture which a people intelligent enough to oppose mass manipulation might have invented. We leave it to them to explain how the historically known practices – which effectively opposed mass manipulation and actually accelerated selection in Nature's direction – might have come into being if not as a culture.

* * *

To keep anyone from organizing a group that could be manipulated to kill individuals, the Northern Europeans adopted a practice of socially approved one-to-one mortal combat. Any person could ask for one-to-one combat with any other person, including a manipulator who tried to form a group to ostracise or kill dissenting individuals. If the would-be manipulator refused to fight on a one-to-one basis, everyone thought of him as a person without honor. No one would then become part of his group and - this is a highly important cultural factor - no woman would want him as the father of her children.

By full social approval of one-to-one combat this culture dealt death in the same selective direction as natural evolution. The one-to-one fights killed off those who wanted a group that - as a group - could be manipulated to overpower and kill off the perceptive individuals who insisted on doing their own thinking.

This bred out cowardly, underhanded, would-be manipulators, and restored the functioning of natural evolution. Without a group that preserved and selectively bred for manipulated zombis, the stupid, who could not survive without someone doing their thinking for them, did not survive.

This culture in Western Asia and Northern Europe also made a point of reversing the group restraint that was practiced in the group-entity cultures regarding a woman's selection of a man for the father of her children.

The group-entity cultures killed women who had sexual relations with any man without group approval. The Northern European culture gave full social approval to a woman's freedom to choose her mate. The people all rejected the idea that any group be allowed to arrogate to itself the power to sanction, or interfere with, a woman's choice of a mate for sexual relations.

There was another important cultural difference affecting a woman's perceptive selection of the father for her children.

Because group-entities were built on "positions" with varying degrees of prestige, those women who got permission from the group to have sexual relations chose men on the basis of their "position" instead of innate qualities.

In the Northern European culture a woman had full freedom of mate-choice, and her perception was not clouded by the "position" a man occupied. There were no "positions," so assessing the innate man was easier. Thus every woman's group-protected-free-will-in-selecting-her mate was a factor of the culture that, like one-to-one combat, went in the same direcion as natural evolution.

These factors of the culture bred for individuals of integrity and sexual perception — as Nature had done before there was any human culture of humans that needed to be opposed.

OPPOSING CULTURES CANNOT BE MIXED

We call the two cultures that breed to develop group-entities the cultures of mass manipulation. We call the one opposing culture the culture of individual sovereignty.

Obviously the cultures that selectively breed in opposite directions cannot be mixed so as to get the "best of each." One will necessarily destroy the other. Any attempt at mixing them can only result in a confusing hodgepodge of ideas that will keep anyone from thinking clearly. A human culture of humans either selectively breeds in the three billion year old direction set by Nature or turns around and goes backward. When the cultural direction is reversed, there may be a static moment, but – like natural evolution – the functioning culture always selectively breeds in a direction that is observable in the universe of time.

Opposing cultures cannot be mixed. But the people bred by the opposing cultures can be mixed. The words and the ideas expressed by the words can be mixed. This confuses clear thought. When the thoughts are confused, people who think for themselves are slow to organize for action. They need time to isolate the problem and to discuss what course of action will best solve it. The mass manipulators, who have bred zombis that act on directions given them in words, take advantage of this and quickly get zombi-action moving in the direction that promotes their culture. They manipulate their masses to overpower open discussion. Thus the culture of individual sovereignty is the one most endangered by mixing people from the opposing cultures.

The individual sovereignty culture that once effectively opposed the zombi-makers has now been rendered ineffective. The mass manipulators are trying to ensure that the very possibility of an alternative to mass manipulation will be forgotten. They talk of culture, itself, as "civilization's refinements," and thereby deflect attention from any thought that human culture of humans is the major, and possibly the only, problem of the human species.

This work focuses on the conflict of opposing cultures. Without challenging the accuracy of accepted history, we will look at the well known facts that are usually called "the rise of Western Civilization." If these facts are viewed without the predilection "the human species has created a great civilization" - if the same facts are examined with the realization that "the human species faces a great problem" - the authors of this work believe that the facts selected for attention outline the problem with a clarity that will encourage consideration of solutions.

The human species has enormous momentum in the direction it is now going, and cannot immediately turn and go in the reverse direction. But possibly it could be stopped before it reaches the point of no return.

Cultures are not natural happenings. Cultures are implemented by human will.

The first step is to discover the source of the will that sets the Nature-opposing direction - and tries to accelerate the Nature-opposing movement.

AN ATTRACTIVE FRONT FOR MASS MANIPULATION

All extant primitive peoples give evidence that, for countless millenniums, manipulated groups have been used to kill off individuals who would not accept direction from the groups' manipulators. At the beginning of the first recorded history of the Western World, some of the Western groups' manipulators had bred up groups that could be manipulated merely by the manipulators' claims in words that they were endowed with some special "authority." Manipulated group force had already done its work in cultural selection.

It is often said that the best way to steer and motivate a jackass is to dangle a carrot before him and hit him from behind with a stick.

In the West, there was a spectacular increase in the size of the manipulated groups when mass produced "carrots" were used to supplement the long used "stick" of manipulated group force.

This increase in the size of manipulated groups helped the culture of mass manipulation to gain dominance over the culture of individual sovereignty.

The current mass manipulators claim that this new use of "carrots" constituted "the beginning of the good life resulting from civilization." Under the word "civilization" they try to lump together things that are not related and thereby cloud perception of what constitutes a "good life." We need to separate unrelated things that have been lumped together.

Mass production of useful things by slaves or by brainwashed zombis and the culture of mass manipulation are essentially related. But overall improvement in the quality of human life is not so related. On the contrary, desirable social relations - mutual love based on perception, and solidly enduring human companionship - are destroyed by the mass manipulation that results in mass production.

When looking at the historical facts, we need to view products that can be made in impressive size or spectacular profusion, and can be used to promote dense populations, as weapons for mass manipulation. That is the way they have always been used or misused.

The distinction between the desirable products created by human ingenuity and the misuse of those products for mass manipulation needs to be crystal clear.

The verbal record of human history that has been twisted by mass manipulators is – at this time – still clear enough that we can, if we choose to do so, look at the known facts.

SUMER

The significant events of the extant Western culture that have been recorded in words begin at the east end of the Mediterranean Sea, in the valley of the Tigris and Euphrates rivers, with a people called the Sumerians. We know very little about these people or the culture that bred them.

It appears that great numbers of the Sumerians had been bred by the culture of mass manipulation that bases "authority" on the purported words of some imaginary god.

The people built canals and used the river water for farming. This productive effort might have started as individual initiative and been imitated by others who saw its value, but the final, big-scale development was clearly dependent on the "god-given authority" that has characterized mass manipulation in the Western World.

The area of these two rivers is now a barren plain that is a swamp at some seasons of the year. What endured were new instruments of mass manipulation.

One was the idea that the culture of mass manipulation could be promoted – more effectively than ever before – by mass producing food to support dense populations. Combined with this was the new idea of money and taxation. This idea we will reserve for fuller examination later on.

Another new instrument of manipulation was the idea that people could be impressed – more effectively than ever before – by awesome tangible evidence that the group is more powerful than the individual.

The people of Sumer, on penalty of death, had to accept the word-stated idea that the manipulators, who made all important decisions for them, were especially chosen by some god for that "position." The people were required to show their acceptance of that idea by building an enormous structure requiring a staggering amount of labor. This was a man-made mountain, terrace after terrace reaching from earth to sky, each smaller than the one below until, finally, it was topped by a temple some 200 by 100 feet.

The physical impressiveness of the structure was combined with the idea that here the manipulators came to have their conferences with the god from whom they purportedly received their "authority."

Two thousand years or so later the Hebrews would record the story of this structure, call it the Tower of Babel, and claim that it ended by breaking the people apart because the Hebrew god made its builders all speak different languages. The contrary result seems to be the valid one. With varying architectural modifications, such as those now found in the cathedrals of Europe, impressive structures have been built in great profusion and used as places for cementing people together by providing them all with the same verbal cliches. The one in Sumer was the prototype of all impressive products of mass human labor that serve to weld people into a group-entity of which all individuals parrot the same words – and obey some "authority" that does their thinking for them.

* * *

This work merely organizes well known information in a way that shows the continuity of cultural directions. The historical events are so widely known that we will not usually clutter up the story's continuity with references. But because we will be considering the influence of the Hebrew and Christian Bibles, we may want to make an occasional reference to these widely distributed publications.

EGYPT

In Egypt the whole Sumerian system was substantially duplicated with conspicuous success. A great devastating flood comes down to us as a tradition from the early days of Sumer. Egypt was free of floods. That advantage was the main difference. The Nile river was used for a group project of building canals that made possible mass produced food to support a dense population. The pyramids, the Sphinx, and the remains of other structures still stand and impress us with the enormous amount of human labor that went into creating this awesome evidence that the group is more powerful than an individual. Herodotus, a Greek historian who lived about 2500 years ago, reported that just one of these structures, the Great Pyramid, required the labor of 100,000 men for twenty years.

The Egyptian manipulators went still further than the Sumerian manipulators in making up fanciful stories as a basis for the idea that the manipulators had special powers to do the people's thinking for them. In Sumer the manipulators merely claimed to be priviledged persons who had conferences with a god. In Egypt it was claimed that the Pharaoh had the privilege of thinking for all the people and telling everybody what to do, because he, himself, was a god. His assistants, who had the job of thinking up impressive stories, admitted that he had a human mother but claimed that he was the son of the sun-god the Egyptians called Ra.

The Sumerian and Egyptian mass manipulators were not the first to claim that they got their "authority" to tell others what to do from some imaginary god. This was a common practice in all the primitive group-entities of the Western World. We are here giving attention to the manipulators in Sumer and Egypt because they added two new weapons to supplement those already used by mass manipulators.

(1) By organizing mass effort for canal building and grain storage, they added "carrots" to the "stick" on which primitive manipulators had relied most heavily.

(2) They had the manipulated people build great stuctures to awe dissenting individuals with the power of a manipulated group.

The massive structures not only impressed the manipulated people, they also impressed the individual sovereignty people with the increasing power of the manipulators over their word-controlled masses.

Perhaps even more impressive to the individual sovereignty people was the increased density of population that resulted from mass produced "carrots." Such dense populations of masses, who let words overrule their perception of reality, could only be seen as a threat to themselves – as people who perceived all Nature as the language of the aboriginal creative consciousness, and, therefore, placed high value on a direct relationship between each individual and the natural world.

CONFLICT BETWEEN CULTURES

There are seemingly endless records of wars between the various groups of mass manipulated people with their different gods and different governments. The recorded details are so many that one could spend a whole lifetime trying to find some significance in them – and then recognize that the time had been wasted. It makes little difference which wins or loses. They are all headed in the way of the regressive insects.

If we don't want to go that way, the only worthwhile information in the word records of humans is the story of conflict between the culture of individual sovereignty and the culture of mass manipulation. This can show how the culture that opposes evolution's long range direction managed to become dominant. This knowledge will help us when we think about what can now be done to re-establish a culture that goes in the three billion year old direction of Nature. In this look at the conflict between the peoples of the opposing cultures, our purpose is to discover what it tells us about the current human problem.

When individual sovereignty people are fighting mass manipulated people, they appear to be no different. They must engage in mass warfare and this requires organized armies. When segregated, when they can avoid any relationship to mass manipulated people, they create no group-entites. Their culture, that gives full social approval to one-to-one combat, prevents manipulated entities from being formed.

As we have noted, there is at present no effectively functioning culture of individual sovereignty. But we want to look at the way it was destroyed so that we can think about how to restore it. We want it primarily because it will give us a better life – allow us, as individuals, to think for ourselves and relate directly to the total universe as individuated units of the aboriginal creative consciousness. But also we want it because, if it could be made worldwide, it would eliminate mass warfare.

In addition to armies of manipulated zombis, mass manipulators use words – not to communicate – but as weapons of warfare. Without discussing cultures – as cultures – they use words to stimulate hatred against the people of the individual sovereignty culture. When they tell anything about the individual sovereignty people, they put emphasis on the well-known ability of the individual sovereignty people as fighters. The mass manipulators try to infer that it is the individual sovereignty people who cause wars.

It is easy to understand why the individual sovereignty people were better fighters than the manipulated masses. Their culture bred for individual courage. But more important, it bred for honesty in their dealings with each other and for love of their comrades. When they fought as armies against mass manipulated armies, they were aware that they were fighting enemies promoting a culture that was designed to destroy what they valued more than life itself – their integrity as individuals. So every individual voluntarily gave his allegiance to his commander for a fight to the death if necessary. When this kind of people opposed what were effectively slave-armies of the mass manipulators, one would logically assume them to be the better fighters – even if six thousand years of history did not demonstrate the fact.

When the picture is the spectacular one of armies fighting armies, the underlying – but all important – conflict of cultures can easily be ignored by those who want to ignore it. In this work the intention is to trace what others have sought to ignore. To do this, we need to identify the individual sovereignty people.

In records that depend on words, people can often be indentified only by their language. The language called Indo-European was the one that generally identified the individual sovereignty people when they first moved into the Mediterranean area and came into conflict with the mass manipulated people. The people speaking the same language also moved into India. In the most ancient Sanskrit writings (the Veda) they call themselves Aryans – meaning excellent or honorable. In the Mediterranean area they called themselves Aryans and gave this name to the area they occupied, Iran (Airyana). In the Hebrew Bible they are called Hittites.

At the time of the first recorded conflict between the

cultures, the Tigris-Euphrates culture had become well defined and well established. Babylon, its center, had become an impressively great city. The form of the group-entity was becoming very clear. A king of Babylonia, Hammurabi, had the "laws," the general orders telling the people what to do and what would happen to them if they did not obey, engraved on a slab of stone about seven feet tall. On the same stone was a picture of the king standing before the sun-god, whom he called Shamash, to receive the laws. These laws in words were very specific. Hammurabi announced in the preamble that god sent "me, Hammurabi, the obedient, god-fearing prince, to make manifest justice in the land, to destroy the wicked and the evildoers, that the strong harm not the weak."

The words of those laws distorted the fact that the manipulated mass was being used to destroy all individuals who insisted on thinking for themselves. Those words - "destroying the wicked and evildoers, that the strong harm not the weak" - set the pattern for distorting facts that has dominated the culture of mass manipulation in the Western World to this day.

The manipulated masses are forced to think and speak in such confused language that, if one tries to talk to them, individuals within the group cannot be reached as individuals speaking a language based on perception of reality. There are no individuals who function as individuals. All have become mere parts of the group-entity. Anyone within the group who opposes the confused, perception-distorting language is called an evildoer to be destroyed. All outside the group who oppose manipulated masses, as such, are called the wicked and the evildoers.

The group-entity thus forces everyone outside the group to deal - not with its component individual parts - but with the whole entity. This gives individual sovereignty people no choice but to band themselves into a fighting force as the only means of effectively opposing the culture.

And even then, words are likely to play into the hands of the group-entity people when individual sovereignty people attempt communication in the confused language of mass manipulation. The Hittites, Aryans, or whatever we call the individual sovereignty people who had established themselves to the north of Babylon, tried using the inacurate language. They said, "If they represent the god of the sun, we should show them what a god of thunder can do." Without realizing that words were weapons, not instruments of communication, among the mass manipulated people, they used such words about gods very casually.

However, they looked to no word-speaking gods to tell them what to do. They thought for themselves and made their own decisions. When they fought, it was not with words used to override clear thought and manipulate people. They used weapons that everyone recognized as weapons. They moved in on Babylon and destroyed it so completely that it was totally ineffective for the next hundred years.

As fighters, they were the best in the area. They brought with them the horse. Faced with the problem of fighting group-entities they developed the cavalry and the light wheeled chariots. An organized army was, of course, necessary when they had to fight a group-entity, and, in meeting that necessity, their organization was good. Administration of a group-entity presented no problem for them. But their culture had always been individual sovereignty. Forming group-entities was not their way of life.

After destroying a group-entity and facing the spectacle of chaos and confusion among the people who were left without anyone to do their thinking for them, the individual sovereignty people again played into the hands of the mass manipulators by using their language. When they had destroyed the manipulators of the people, an unsought power incidentally fell into their hands: The conquered people thought of their conquerors as kings to be obeyed without question. So the individual sovereignty people began taking on ruling roles and titles that the conquered people understood.

They recognized the danger of doing this, so the kings set up councils to whom they voluntarily gave power to execute themselves if they got carried away from their cultural heritage by the power that incidentally fell into their hands. Also, following their tradition of formal one-to-one combat, they began the practice of making formal declarations of war. Additionally, a king, instead of using his "position" to command obedience, often told a subordinate what he did not like about his administration and, if there was no agreement, the king, himself, would propose that they let a fight make the decision.

But there is no way to amalgamate diametrically opposing cultures. In an area dominated by group-entities, individuals have no chance of practicing their own culture. And there can be no compromise between cultures.

The individual sovereignty people did not lose the fight in the Mediterranean area because they were "a bunch of barbarians opposing the rise of civilzation." They did not fail to establish a group-entity superior to the others because they lacked the ability. They did not do so because group-entities were not compatible with their culture of individual sovereignty. It was the culture, not the niceties of "civilization," that the fight was about. And we who want to restore the culture of individual sovereignty can only continue to look at what happened with the hope of avoiding past mistakes.

After destroying Babylon, these people that the Bible calls Hittites gradually became intermixed with the group-entity people and their culture was never effectively established. The widow of an Egyptian Pharaoh, almost certainly Tutankhamen, impressed by the quality of these people, married a son of one of their kings. Respect for the Hittites was obviously marked in Egypt, because later a Pharaoh married a Hittite princess.

However Egypt was also a product of the mass manipulation culture and the individual sovereignty people wanted no part of the culture as such. About three thousand years ago the Hittites fought the Egyptians to a standstill and a major treaty was made between Ramses of Egypt and Hattusilis III that lasted for seventy years.

Wave after wave of the individual sovereignty people continued to enter the Mediterranean area through the Iranian plateau. And wave after wave of them was mixed with the group-entity people. Still they kept coming – and still they tried to use words to reason with people who had become zombis. .... Zombis, the living dead, is the only fitting description for people who have been brainwashed to the point where they can be fully controlled by mere words that come from outside themselves.

Over a thousand years after Hammurabi recorded words that he said came from god, the individual sovereignty people were still trying to use the the twisted words of the manipulated masses to point out to them the "wrong" done by their "holy" words. Darius, the leader of a new wave of people who thought for themselves, proud that he was, in his words, "an Aryan having Aryan lineage" – but faced with the word lineage of Hammurabi – made known his view in the "holy" words of Hammurabi by saying "it is not my desire that the weak man should have wrong done to him by the strong, nor is it my desire that the strong man should have wrong done to him by the weak."

THE MAKING OF A GROUP-ENTITY

The feature of the Western manipulated mass culture that distinguishes it from that of the Orient is the use of complicated, confused, and often meaningless words. The bare preamble to Hammurabi's laws is enough to identify the pattern of twisted words used by the mass manipulators in the West. But we can follow the development of the Western form of the culture most readily by looking at the actual replacement of Hammurabi's initial code. This replacement is still current and has been the focal point of the West's cultural conflict. Many details about its origin have come down to us in words and a review of these details will help clarify the total picture.

About thirty-three hundred years ago, a people, whose language was a division of the Semitic called Hebrew, and who, as a people, are often called Hebrews, were part of the Egyptian Empire. It is often said that they were "slaves" of the Egyptians. Their Bible makes it clear that they were intermediates between the Egyptians and the slaves. The Hebrews administered over the Egyptian slaves. They had individual slaves that they considered their property and which they took with them when they became a separate group-entity.

There is a long story in their Bible of how, in anticipation of what would happen, they "borrowed" much jewelry and valuables from the Egyptians. They then accelerated the sabatoge they had been carrying on until they were driven out of Egypt. Moses, who had been the leader of the sabotage activity, was then faced with the problem of what to do when the Hebrews were a large group with no experience in living as a separate people.

They had already been conditioned to live within a group-entity, and apparently had long been culturally bred for that life. Living as sovereign individuals appears to have been inconceivable to them. They knew only how to live as a group-entity. They also knew, and obviously approved of, the practices that led to the establishment of the Western World's group-entities. So they offer us a historical example of exactly how the West's group-entities were formed.

They were just a large group of people, with their cattle, their slaves, and their "borrowed" gold, jewelry and valuables, out in the desert. They were already a "civilized" people that we can look at as a group willfully forming a group-entity.

The detailed story provides an opportunity for viewing a group-entity formation as something separate from the niceties that are claimed to be the mark distinguishing the "civilized" from the "barbarians." Aside from the clothes on their backs, their domesticated cattle, their slaves, and their "borrowed" valuables, they had only one heritage from "civilization." They had been verbally conditioned to think of themselves as a group-entity.

They were free but they resented freedom. They complained to Moses that all he had done was bring them out into the desert to starve and they wished that they were back. He set about making use of their group-entity conditioning.

Moses had no impressive man-made mountain such as the Sumerians had built, with a temple on top, where the manipulators claimed that they got the "authority" for what they wanted to do from a god. But he followed the practice that had worked in Sumer. He went up on a mountain to impress the people that he was getting special instructions from a god. He did not have good craftsmen to do his bidding but, after forty days, he came down with a slab of stone with ten of the Hammurabi-type laws on it.

Even after twenty-seven hundred years of "civilization" that selected only the brainwashed for survival, some of the people were not as fully conditioned as Moses might have expected. Some ridiculed what he had done. So he had to do some additional cultural selecting. According to Exodus 32:26-28, here is what happened:

Moses said, "Who is on the LORD's side? . . . And all the sons of Levi gathered themselves together unto him. And he said unto them. Thus saith the LORD God of Israel, Put every man his sword by his side, and go in and out from gate to gate throughout the camp, and slay every man his brother, and every man his companion, and every man his neighbor. And the children of Levi did according to the word of Moses, and there fell of the people that day about three thousand men."

Moses was working on the conditioning of the people without any impressive structures and without any group constructed canals that were a benefit of "civilization" that all could see. So he brought forth a statement that his god was jealous of other gods, that his god wanted no graven images of himself, that his god wanted no impressive man made mountain such as the Sumerians had built – that his god had even brought a curse upon the Sumerian people who thought they could build a temple reaching from earth to the sky.

Later there would be less talk of being jealous of other gods, and the claim would be made by the Hebrews that their god was the only god, the actual creator of heaven and earth. Future writers would add such extravagant embellishments to the god being created out of words. But for the moment there were more practical matters pressing on the mass manipulator.

If the group-entity was to survive as such, it needed to have a way to live. Moses brought the word, which he claimed came from god, that it should live on the milk and honey produced by other people.

A GROUP-ENTITY WITHOUT ADORNMENT

Human group-entities are formed by combining force and twisted words in a way that overrules individual thought. Hammurabi said that his "laws from god" were for the purpose of keeping the strong from harming the weak. As demonstrated in practice, they were for the purpose of using a manipulated mass against those who cherished their individual integrity and wanted to think for themselves. One of the Hammurabi-type "laws from god" that Moses brought down from the mountain was "Thou shalt not kill." But he immediately demonstrated that it meant: You shall not make your own decisions about who needs to be killed; you shall let the spokesman for the group-entity do your thinking and make all decisions about killing for you.

Because mortal conflict is a condition inseparable from existence as a living thing, when group-entities take over direct relationship to the universe from individuals, mass warfare is inevitable. Since the Hebrews were already conditioned to think of themselves as parts of a group-entity and, since the purported word from their god was that they should live off the milk and honey produced by other group entities, mass warfare was a condition to which they were committed. They knew it. But there was a problem.

In the specialization that had taken place within the long-established Egyptian group-entity, they had not been selected and brought into the Egyptian Empire to be the fighter class. Nor had they been selectively bred for it during the four hundred years they had been there. They had been intermediates between the ruling class and the slaves. Intrigue, the petty pomposity of mid-level people seeking "higher positions," and the ability to twist words - these were the skills they had learned. They lacked enough men of courage, with faithfulness to their ideals and their comrades, to get the milk and honey of others by open attack. They turned to the weapons they knew: Their mass warfare was conspicuously characterized by emphasis on falseness, twisted words, and deceit.

Whenever they could they infiltrated other group-entities and killed them off without open fights. For some three hundred years, they did not openly declare themselves a group-entity by using the word "king" to identify the manipulator of their new entity. They called their internal rulers "priests" and "judges" instead of "kings." Saul was first to take the title of king. This was their first honest declaration that, three hundred years before, they had entered the arena of group-entities.

At the time of Saul, their major enemy was a settlement of what the Bible calls Philistines. We are not positive just who these Philistines were. The names of their towns were Semitic, but they may simply not have bothered to change the names given to them by others. They clearly were not native to the area because they were called "the sea people." From their customs as recited in the Bible, we can assume that they were products of the individual sovereignty culture. The Bible tells of one of them, described as a "giant," who came out and dared any man in all of Saul's kingdom to meet him in one-to-one combat. A shepherd boy, David, who had developed skill in the use of the sling, made an impression - apparently on both the Hebrews and the Philistines - by having the courage to meet this "giant" Philistine. He hit him in the head with a rock from his sling, knocked him out, then took the Philistine's own sword and cut off his head. David became a hero in the eyes of the Hebrews and King Saul was jealous of him.

David developed, or for purposes of deceiving the Philistines appeared to develop, a mortal enmity with King Saul. He joined the Philistines and they accepted him as one of their army leaders. He said that he wanted to help in the leadership of the Philistine armies against the Hebrews. The Philistine's top leader was willing to accept him, but the council, that could overrule leaders when the people were dealing with group-entities, would not permit it. They suspected David's sincerity and thought he would betray the Philistines in the middle of the battle.

Later events showed that the Philistines were right in suspecting that David would betray them. David followed Saul as king of the Hebrews and, with his knowledge of the Philistines' layout and ways of battle, he began to build a full-fledged kingdom.

In building his kingdom, David had the help of an unstated number of Hittites – the individual sovereignty people who called themselves Aryans. They must have been well established among the Hebrews for they were close enough to the palace that King David noticed the wife of one of them taking a bath and decided he must have her. Her husband was helping David fight his battles. David conspired to have him placed in the front of a battle, without support, and be killed. Then David had a son by the Hittite woman. This son, Solomon – who was half a product of the mass manipulation culture and half a product of the individual sovereigty culture – became king after David.

Under King Solomon the kingdom of the Hebrews had what was later referred to as its period of glory. Aside from this brief period of "glory," the Hebrew story shows a group-entity that repeated all the characteristics of the Sumerians and the Egyptians except that it provided no tangible products of "civilization." From the beginning it set out to live on the niceties of "civilization" produced by others – what the spokesman for its god called the milk and honey.

We have gone into some detail because this group-entity gives us a background for a specific conflict that can be traced to the present time. This conflict points up the difference between the simple brainwashing in the Orient and the more complex brainwashing in the Western World. From the full story we can learn how the culture of mass manipulation came to dominate the Western World.

Although we know that King Solomon was half Aryan, we cannot be sure just how much interbreeding between products of the mass manipulation culture and the individual sovereignty culture the Hebrew method of waging war by infiltration and deceit had resulted in by King Solomon's time. However, we do know that, of the original twelve tribes of Hebrews, only the tribe of Judah remained together. Thereafter the Hebrews of the tribe of Judah called themselves the Jews, and when those from any of the other tribes rejoined them they, too, were called Jews.

This group-entity, now called Jewish, but having continuity from the Hebrew entity formed by Moses to live off the milk and honey of others, continues to the present day. It gives us a clear picture of a primitive group-entity, before the Sumerians and Egyptians began using the "carrots" produced by the manipulated mass as weapons for further manipulation. It gives us a picture of a group-entity that is a group-entity - and nothing else.

SOME ATTEMPTS TO MIX CULTURES

Separation of opposing cultures is necessary if the culture of individual sovereignty is to survive.

When individual sovereignty people must fight the mass manipulated people who threaten to absorb or destroy them, they have no choice but to form organized armies. Such an army is really a temporary group-entity of those defending individual sovereignty. For the duration of the fight, individual sovereignty must be suspended and everyone must obey the tactical orders of the group's commander. If the mass manipulated people are a dense population pressing in from all sides, if the individual sovereignty people cannot quickly achieve full victory and again segregate themselves, if mobilization must extend beyond the army to the whole people and continue for generations, then their temporary group-entity has become a permanent one. Their way of life is gone. There is no longer a distinction between their way of life and that of the mass manipulated people.

This is what happened to all the waves of individual sovereignty people who went into the Mediterranean area of Northern Africa. With a different spelling, Iran (Land of the Aryans) still bears their name, but their culture has disappeared.

* * *

The individual sovereignty people went into India with very much the same result. The thought pattern on which their commitment to individual sovereignty was based is still identifiable in the Hindu religion but it has been distorted and deprived of its original clarity. Perception that saw purpose in life was distorted into a religion of retreat from a life so mired in the remains of a long enduring culture of mass manipulation that its purpose was no longer perceivable.

Life's purpose and direction needs no explanation. It only needs innate perception that is unclouded by words. The attempt to rationalize opposition to life's purpose and direction can never find enough words to be fully convincing. In India the people still keep talking.

What became an involved religion in India was originally merely the assumptions that followed logically from innate perception. Because everyone recognized a perceptive intelligence in himself, it was assumed to have come from an aboriginal perceptive intelligence. Since everyone could see that living things had to fight each other for living room, those who consciously recognized their individual sovereignty concluded that opposing individuals should be viewed as the thoughts and words of the aboriginal intelligence being weighed against each other. Therefore integrity and courage in the fight was the role of high honor to be played by individual descendants of the aboriginal creative intelligence who had reached the plateau of perception where they could view the whole. The overall decision was manifest as the continuing reality. It was important to look carefully at all Nature if one hoped to perceive reality's long range direction.

In India the Aryans faced an enormous mass of group-entity people. They became mired in the mass that had been conditioned by long manipulation, and began to think that their individual beings were a hopeless mistake. They had too much perception to accept the group-entity way of life. They decided that each individual should seek to uncreate himself by undoing all he had ever done. The objective of this was to again become an undivided part of the aboriginal consciousness.

* * *

When the individual sovereignty people went into Greece they were able to achieve total dominance of a limited area. But they recognized that their limited area could not be fully segregated. They recognized that they had moved into a world of group-entities.

They also recognized that, in a world of group-entities, some sort of laws were necessary for people accustomed to being manipulated by laws. The adminstrative system that the group-entities used to implement the "words from their gods" was called a government. The Greeks, with their individual sovereignty background, said that they would have a "scientific government" made up of voluntary agreements betweeen sovereign individuals.

The "scientific government" was conceived as being based on individuals of unshakable integrity. The individual sovereignty idea was that all relationships must be voluntary. Voluntary implies an acceptable alternative. The Greeks based their government on the idea that those who did not want to participate could and would leave.

But when the individual sovereignty people took over Greece, they found a population that had not been bred for unshakable integrity. The native people could not participate in a government based on such a premise. They were accustomed to obeying "authority" and had no concept of how to live without it. They showed themselves willing to accept any designated "authority." The individual sovereignty people decided the native people could be useful and allowed them to remain as slaves. The slaves had no voice in the government but the "citizens" and "slaves" got along well.

However, daily association with those bred by the mass manipulation culture had its effect on the Greeks. They invented a whole imaginary world of gods as people invent fairy stories. Some of the people came to believe that these gods actually existed. But for several hundred years the Greeks, with their "scientific" government – and their individual sovereignty background – had what appears to have been a very pleasant life.

About twenty-three hundred years ago a Greek, Alexander the Great, conquered the whole Mediterranean area and set up Greek cities designed to be examples of Greek thought and the Greek way of living. This enabled the mass manipulated people to see a way of life that appeared better than their own. The hope was that the manipulated people would all see the value of the individual sovereignty culture and adopt it. This did not work. The people bred for mass manipulation had no will to change.

The Romans took over the whole pantheon of gods the Greeks had invented, used it as the mass manipulated people had always used their gods – to awe and control people with mystery and "authority." Then, pragmatically using people bred for mass manipulation rather than trying to change them, the Romans took over the whole Mediterranean area that Alexander had conquered.

During the period of Roman control, a significant event

provided the mixed people of the Mediterranean area with a statement – made in the crystal clear language of reality – that the conflict between the opposing cultures is mortal and eternal.

WORDS USED TO COMMUNICATE
AND
WORDS AS WEAPONS OF DESTRUCTION

For a period of two or three hundred years, beginning about two thousand years ago, it appeared as if the issue between the individual sovereignty people and the mass manipulated people – the problem of the whole human species – had been stated so clearly that even the manipulated people could see what was happening to them. One sovereign individual called Jesus conspicuously set himself in opposition to the culture of mass manipulation and exposed its falsity and destructiveness for all to see.

Jesus was born in the middle of a bitter conflict between two formal implements of mass manipulation – the Roman group-entity and the Jewish group-entity. And he was born in an area where there still remained thirteen cities set up by Alexander as examples of the Greek way of life and Greek thought.

The Greek examples carried some of the original thoughts of the individual sovereignty people. The original thought pattern had become confused by mixing the people from two opposing cultures. However, an individual with clear perception could see the basic conflict between opposing cultures. Jesus saw this. He also saw that, if it was not stopped, the culture of mass manipulation would destroy the human species.

It would appear to be no random accident that Jesus, who saw the problem so clearly, was born among the Jews. Their group-entity was the clearest possible example of the problem because it had been least confused with "the niceties of civilization." The Jewish manipulators offered their people no products of "civilization" created by the joint efforts of those in their group-entity. Moses had merely offered them the choice: Accept the god I tell you about and accept me as his spokesman or simply tell me that you do not. Then – without warning them what he planned to do, without giving them a chance to defend themselves – he immediately demonstrated that those who did not accept would be killed by those who did.

That set the pattern for Judaism. The Jews tried to hide what they were doing behind an elaborate rattle of words, and sought to confuse people regarding their intentions. But when they thought the time was ripe for action, their actions were the essense of the mass manipulation culture in its stark primitive nakedness.

In the area where Jesus was born, everyone had to be part of some group-entity. The only question among the Jews was whether to be a part of the Roman entity or the Jewish entity. Some tried to be parts of both. What had already been reduced to nothing but part of a group-entity, they tried to split. They lived in a world of words rather than a world of Nature or reality. They did not think of all this as attempts to mutilate their natural beings. They thought of it as being "civilized."

The Jews, Romans, and everyone in the Mediterranean area, had been conditioned to measure an individual's worth by the "position" he held in a group-entity. All accepted the conditioning that one who was not part of a group-entity had no worth. The thoughts that Jesus expressed were the thoughts of the individual sovereignty people:

Because each individual recognized perceptive intelligence in himself, the individual sovereignty people had concluded that it came from an aboriginal perceptive intelligence. Jesus used the word "Father" for this aboriginal perceptive intelligence. He recognized it as existing in all living things. He told people to consider the lillies of the field and notice that Solomon in all his glory had no more beautiful clothes than they. He pointed out that, in the commercial values of group-entities, sparrows were sold at two for a penny – and yet each individual sparrow was cherished by the Father. Then, he said, if a sparrow had worth in the thoughts of the Father, an individual human must have much more.

With regard to the relations of individuals to the group-entities that were in conflict with each other, he told the people to take no sides. Each group-entity demonstrated its power by fighting the other. If an individual opposed one, that opposition was a help to the other. He said that if the Jewish tax collector took away your coat, let him have it, and let him have your overcoat too. If a Roman soldier told you to go along with him and carry his pack for one mile, do it, and carry it a second mile if necessary to show your lack of opposition. Opposition to one group-entity was help and support to another.

He tried to avoid all subjects where his words could be twisted to mean that he was on one side or the other. He avoided the question of whether Jews should pay taxes to the Romans, instead of tithes to their Jewish god, by merely saying, "Render unto Caesar the things that are Caesar's and unto God the things that are God's." He saved a woman who had not followed the Jewish entity's demand that no woman could have sexual relations without authorization from the Jewish group-entity - and did it in such a way that he did not challenge the laws supposedly given to Moses by the Jewish god. He was not yet ready for a confrontation.

His positive statements all supported these basic ones: He said "I am in the Father and the Father in me. If you have seen me you have seen the Father." He used the term "Holy Spirit" to talk of the Father within one as distinguished from a man-invented god whom manipulators presented as speaking human words. He used the term "kingdom of heaven" to talk of how things should be without the group-entities that people had created. He said that knowledge of the Father and of the kingdom of heaven was within everyone. He said that, if people were going to pray, that prayer should be something done alone and it should be that the will of the Father be done on earth as it was in the kingdom of heaven. He said that the kingdom of heaven was not a location; that it was within one. He told people that they could go against the law and that was not important, they could go against what they called "god" and that was not important, but if they opposed the Holy Spirit that was within them they would be eternally damned.

In words, there can be no clearer statement of the basis on which the culture of individual sovereignty was built. But Jesus wanted to make a clearer statement than words can make.

He prepared himself to make that clearer statement. He lived without doing anything in direct opposition to either the laws of the Jews or the laws of the Romans. The Romans could not openly execute him as a breaker of Roman law. And the Jews could not use the practice that the Romans let them get by with - the practice of stoning the breakers of Jewish "laws from god" to death in some back alley.

Because the Jews were under Roman law, Jesus could force a publicly viewed confrontation – one that would be between group-entities in general and an individual who had done nothing in opposition to any group-entity but proclaim his individual sovereignty.

He knew that such a confrontation would bring the conflict between sovereign individuals and group-entities out into the open. Thereafter, all who proclaimed their individual sovereignty would be branded as enemies by the group-entities. They would have to fight for bare survival. He told his disciples, "Sell your coat and buy a sword."

He picked the time of the Passover, when the Jews celebrated the beginning of the Jewish group-entity, for the confrontation. He knew that they would not ignore open defiance at the time of their most "holy" celebration.

The Jews arrested him, and brought him before the Roman governor. The Roman governor found him innocent of any wrongdoing. But the Jews demanded that he be crucified. The Romans finally consented.

Almost immediately after the crucifixion, everyone recognized that, by his public trial and death on the cross, Jesus – one sovereign individual – had won a victory over both the Jewish group-entity and the Roman group-entity. Because he had not broken the laws of either, his crucifixion had shown, with a clarity that could no longer be ignored, that the conflict between individuals who merely upheld their inborn sovereignty and all group-entities was mortal and eternal. There could be no compromise. Every individual must make a choice between the two opposing cultures.

Jesus had taught that a living individual has more value than one who is a mere part of a group-entity – no matter what "position" in the group-entity the part occupies. His message was that those who obeyed mere words were damned – that those who obeyed the law and the prophets were already dead. To enter the kingdom of heaven they would have to leave the manipulated mass and the laws that overrode individual will. The change was as great as if they were being reborn. He taught that an individual who wanted to be a living thing had to obey only the Holy Spirit within himself.

Many began to take courage from the courage he had shown. They openly identified themselves as followers of Jesus and were called Christians. They banded together to discuss his teachings and consider what strategy they should adopt.

At first the Roman Empire was considered by its rulers as too big and powerful to become much concerned. The Roman rulers decided to leave the problem to the Jews. The Jews were the ones who had cried out, "Crucify him."

The Jews tried to stop the opposition that the crucifixion had aroused to Judaism. The Roman practice was to allow Jews to kill off – by back alley gang tactics – those who showed disregard for the laws that they claimed came from their god. The Romans gave the Jewish gangs a free hand with regard to the Christians.

The leader of one such gang, Saul of Tarsus, becomes very important in our story as an example of how words can be used to twist and distort clear thought. (Saul was one of those who tried to play it safe by being a part of both entities. Paul was his name as a part of the Roman entity.)

The body of Jesus had already been crucified. But the spirit of Jesus, or memory of what he had said and done, lived on. Paul used words to crucify the spirit of Jesus.

By the use of words, Paul turned the whole meaning of what Jesus had done backwards. He invented a meaning for the crucifixion opposite to what Jesus had taught in words – and what Jesus had so clearly shown by the courageous act of putting himself in the position where he would be crucified.

Paul used words to destroy the eloquent statement Jesus made by avoiding the usual Jewish method of a back alley stoning. He invented a false explanation for the obvious fact that Jesus had deliberately invited a public trial and crucifixion: The Jews had a practice of killing an animal on an altar. They called it "a sacrifice for their sins." Sin was the word they used to mean disobeying the laws that they claimed came from the god they had invented. Paul said that when Jesus talked about the "Father" he meant the Jewish god. Paul then claimed that the crucifixion of Jesus had been the Jewish god sacrificing his own son for the sins of all the people who had not obeyed the Jewish laws.

It would be difficult to describe in words the significance of what Paul did more effectively than Nietzsche did in his book, "The Anti-Christ." He said that Paul nailed Jesus back on the cross.

Paul set up a chain of churches and began to use the story of Jesus he had invented in the same way the Sumerians and Egyptians had used the sun god, and the Jews had used the god they invented – to give "authority" to the words of the one who claimed to be the god's spokesman.

But in spite of Paul and his chain of churches, the real story of Jesus was still told for about three hundred years. Real Christians continued to band together for strength.

Three hundred years after Jesus, Christians, in increasing numbers, were becoming a problem to the Roman Empire.

The anti-Christ groups that Paul had built up also called themselves "Christians." This use of the same word to identify two cultures that were in mortal opposition caused a lot of confusion. The confusion was intensified because some people tried to coodinate the opposing ideas. All together there were over a hundred different sects. These included some attempted mixings between the groups of anti-Christ "Christians" that Paul had built up and real Christians. As always happens, the attempted mixings played into hands of the manipulators.

Apparently the real Christians, those actually following the teachings of Jesus, were beginning to take the advice Jesus gave to his disciples, "Sell your coat and buy a sword." They were becoming a problem to the Romans. We know there is a twisted story about "George the dragon slayer" that never makes it quite clear what group-entity the dragon was. It might even have been one of the anti-Christ "Christian" sects that were trying to destroy the real Christians. Important facts about the story were apparently suppressed until they were wiped out of histories. But we know that the word "dragon" is used in Northern European mythology to mean group-entity. We know that "dragon" is even used throughout the Bible to mean group-entity. And we know that George was a real man, a Christian, a soldier, and that he was captured and tortured by the Roman Emperor Diocletian, and was put to death by the Emperor on April 23, 303 A.D. in Nicomedia.

In 314 A.D. the Roman Emperor Constantine convened a council to study the various teachings of all the Christian sects. In 325 A.D. he convened another council and selected one for recognition by the Roman Empire as the "official Christianity," with the understanding that it would either absorb or destroy the others.

With some modifications to make the story of Jesus that Paul had invented go even further in portraying Jesus as a group-entity god, the anti-Christ "Christianity" of Paul was the one selected.

The anti-Christ "Christianity" of Paul was used to destroy the real Christians within the Roman Empire. After that it was used to destroy the whole individual sovereignty culture in Northern Europe that had withstood all the power the Roman armies had been able to bring against it.

It was fifteen hundred years before a President of the United States, Thomas Jefferson, removed the twisted words in which the story of Jesus had been inbedded. During those years inquisitions of the Catholic Church had used a combination of force and words to make a whole people accept and teach their children the recognizably false Judaeo-"Christianity" invented by Paul. Cutting away the obvious falsity that the manipulators had injected into the Bible, Jefferson said that the true story of Jesus was "as easily distinguised as diamonds in a dung-hill."

A COMBINATION OF MISUSED WORDS AND FORCE

If we looked only at what is now called Christianity, we would find it inconceivable that the Northern Europeans would have allowed that "Christianity's" priests to infiltrate their homeland. It, therefore, appears highly probable that the true story of Jesus had been spread among the Northern Europeans during the three hundred years before the real Christians were destroyed by the "official Christianity" of the Roman Empire. There is no other way to account for the initial acceptance of the priests bearing the mass manipulation story invented by Paul.

Even so, the priests would have had to continue using the true story to gain entrance to the Northern European area. Only when they had built up a group they could control, could they gradually twist the story to the one Paul had invented.

In order to understand why the priests could use the true story of Jesus to gain acceptance, it is necessary to remove a falsification of facts that has been promoted by mass manipulators and is still widely accepted. Against conclusive evidence of falsity, it is still widely accepted that the Northern Europeans were barbarians worshiping many strange gods. Julius Caesar, who fought them, studied their ways, and wrote the only firsthand information we have about them, said that those east of the Rhine (the ones that are still there and those that are now the English, Americans, and Scandinavians) had no gods of the kinds other people had, that they looked directly to Nature as the source of all benefits. He emphasized that they had no priests or druids like those of Romanized Gaul.

Looking at the early religions of Greece and India that derive from the same common source, we know that the whole culture of the Northern Europeans was based on belief in one aboriginal creative consciousness that continues in every living thing.

The Roman priests gained admittance among the Northern Europeans by describing Jesus as one who believed as they did. They quoted the statements he had made that heaven was within, that he was in the Father and the Father was in him, that all living things were cherished children of the Father, even the lillies of the field and the birds in the air. And they told of a Jesus who, like all the Northern Europeans, lived and died with integrity and courage. They told of a Jesus, who weaponless had defied the group-entity people and had died as bravely as all the Northern European heroes who had fought the dragons, or group-entities.

These Northern Europeans had long been threatened by the "dragons" (the manipulated group-entities) outside their area. Their life in harmony with Nature had been disturbed by the necessity for organizing armies to oppose the group-entity people.

From the area of the group-entity people, now came priests saying that they represented some among the group-entity people who wanted to stop the long standing conflict - who even had a law "Thou shalt not kill."

Like Moses, the priests were merely trying to lure the people into a false sense of security until a manipulated group could be formed among them that would accept the interpretation: "Thou shalt not kill until ordered to do so by an 'authorized spokesman' for the group-entity."

As long as anyone could remember the policy of the individual sovereignty people had been "kill the dragons" and uphold the "fair fight" (one-to-one) combat that keeps manipulated group-entities from being formed among us. Accepting priests, who falsely said that they represented people who did not want to kill the individual sovereignty people, was accepting camouflaged dragon seeds planted among them.

The dragon seeds planted among the individual sovereignty people were nourished by an elaborate organization among the group-entity people outside the area. The Catholic Church had a strategy planning staff and the priests were schooled in tactical maneuvers.

When the priests got enough followers they began subtly twisting the story until they had identified the anti-Christ "Christians" who were following the teachings of

Paul with the real Christians who were following the teachings of Jesus. After the one word, "Christian," had been used for three hundred years to mean the people of two cultures that mortally opposed each other, the priests saw what clever tricks can be played with words.

The priests performed Paul's word trick again. They said that the "Father" of Jesus, and the "aboriginal creative consciousness" of the Northern European were all just different words for the "god" of the Jews.

This word trick was aided by the fact that the Northern Europeans and the priests had a clear cut point of full agreement: They both fully rejected the multiple gods of the Romans.

Once the Jewish tribal god was accepted as being the same as the aboriginal creative consciousness, there remained only the matter of getting the people to accept the priests' assertions that this one and only god had told the Jews to write down some laws in words.

As soon as the priests had a group that would obey "authoritative" words, they used the group to overpower, torture, and kill those who would not let words overrule the perception that was within them.

Finally the priests got some of the Northern Europeans, themselves, to create group-entities. They used the same misleading words that Moses had used: "Thou shalt not kill" and omitted the underhanded part – unless you are told to kill by a spokesman with "authority." Like the people manipulated by Moses, the Northern Europeans began obeying the "authority" and went about killing every man his brother, his companion, and his neighbor who would not accept words from the spokesman for the man-invented god as more important than their own perception. When the culture of mass manipulation got into full swing, millions upon millions of the individual sovereignty people were killed by their former comrades.

In addition to the misuse of words in combination with force, a misuse of money helped the mass manipulators to destroy the individual sovereignty people. Julius Caesar said that the Northern Europeans knew about money but did not use it and did not want to use it. When the ways of the group-entity people were imposed on them, the use of money was part of those ways. They became dependent on it, as all group-entity people do.

An exceptional tricky use of money became one of the methods the priests put into effect to destroy the practice of socially approved one-to-one combat that the Northern Europeans had depended on to maintain their individual sovereignty culture.

A group-entity is based on the idea of "positions of authority" - different degrees of sovereignty. The idea that "positions of authority" exist independent of the individuals occuping the "positions" is an essential factor of the group-entity concept. The idea must be accepted that a king, a priest, or any other mass manipulator may be a fallible human but a "position of authority" is a necessity because group-entities are a necessity. The fallible human only has "authority" because he occupies a "position of authority." The "position" becomes the important thing.

One of the tactics the priests used to destroy the culture of individual sovereignty was inventing "classes" of people claimed to have "different degrees of sovereignty." Among the Northern Europeans, the priests pushed for a division of people into those who had the "right" to one-to-one combat and those who did not. Nobility and honor were ideas the people used to describe admirable individuals. The priests began talking of the "nobles" and the "common people" as "classes" or "positions."

To promote the idea, money was injected to help confuse the thought pattern.

The priests, who themselves had been required to respond to challenges for one-to-one combat or lose respect, came up with the idea that the "upper classes" need not respond to challenges from the "lower classes" - that, instead of giving satisfaction by one-to-one combat, payment of money for the harm done was an honorable settlement.

Money, which 3,500 years before had been invented as a weapon intrinsically favorable to mass manipulators, has many facets that give advantage to mass manipulators.

When the idea was injected and accepted that money could buy off the age-old social agreement that promoted the individual sovereignty culture of the people - the agreement that any individual could demand and receive satisfaction for any offense against him on "the field of honor" – the culture of mass manipulation had taken over Northern Europe.

MONEY

Current mass manipulators carefully promote the less than half truth that money is merely a medium of exchange.

If there were any occasion for the use of money within a culture of individual sovereignty, money would be a medium of exchange and only that. But in a worldwide culture of sovereign individuals there would be no occasion to use money. The early Northern Europeans rejected its use. The early Greeks compromised; they used money but made a point of ensuring that their money was in a form not acceptable in trade outside their own realm.

The purposes of money other than its use as a mere medium of exchange are what vitally concern us.

Money was conceived and created as a weapon of mass manipulation. In Sumer, useful products became a "carrot" of mass manipulation that supplemented the "stick" of manipulated group force. Money was invented because the manipulators needed to devise a way to fine tune their control over the useful products.

From primitive times they had manipulated a word controlled group powerful enough to take everything from those who would not submit to word control. Now they decided that they would not take everything from dissenting individuals; they would take only a portion of what these individuals produced so as to encourage them to keep producing. This restraint on how much they took would lull those who could not be controlled by words into passive acceptance of the manipulators' - only partially used - group-entity power. This system of making power inconspicuous and encouraging continued production by taking only a portion of what is produced is called taxation.

A convenient unit of measure for the new idea of taxation was needed. That is the origin and the original purpose of money.

A standard measure of grain was the first money. But collecting tax in measures of grain, or a percentage of one's cattle, was too cumbersome for the mass manipulators. At that time metal was new, rare, and prized. It had intrinsic value. In Sumer, about 4500 years ago, the manipulators began to replace measures of grain with pieces of metal as money. Taxes were imposed in coined money.

Coined money quickly came to represent the force of the manipulators. They began to require that taxes be paid in a piece of metal with the image of the "Caesar" on it. To get the money to pay taxes one had to participate in the increasingly complex system of mass manipulation. Payment in coined money - the use of which was an unspoken token of submission to measured force - staved off the use of still greater force.

The image of the "Caesar" - not the intrinsic value of the metal - soon came to be the important thing. Everyone had to deal in the "coin of the realm." Accepting the use of money was accepting one's dependence on, and submission to, the power held by the realm's mass manipulators.

A significant aspect of money - which manipulators are careful to omit from the school book definition - is our major concern. It can be simply stated: A unit of money is a unit of manipulated force that belongs to the force-controller whose stamp is on the money.

The basic force behind the culture of mass manipulation is a word controlled group used as a weapon against any individual who opposes the manipulators. Initially the force is expressed by killing and physical torture. As the culture gains in power the mere threat of killing, physical torture, or even imprisonment, is sufficient to enforce submission to manipulation.

Then, as mass manipulation is accepted as the only way of life, becoming one of the manipulators begins to appear more desirable than submitting to manipulation. Acceptance by the manipulated group - and status, "a position" within the group - is actively sought. Money comes to be a symbol of status. Money becomes "position" in the abstract, or an instrument for acquiring a "position."

As people ponder the myriad ways that money can be used and misused, the idea is likely to develop that money is power in the abstract. It is not. It is the power of the manipulators whose stamp is on it.

The idea that money is power in the abstract often leads those who oppose mass manipulation to think that enough money will restore their individual sovereignty. It will not.

Ignorance of this fact induces those with much money to hug to themselves the illusion that they, and their friends who also have great amounts of money and so make up a sort of exclusive society, have already reclaimed their individual sovereignty. They have not. Money can only buy for them the fawning, pseudo-respect that brainwashed zombis give to their "sovereigns" - those who hold the "highest positions" in the hierarchy of manipulators.

The illusion that individual sovereignty can come from enough money keeps the people who have the time and ability to do something effective toward establishing, or re-establishing, the culture of individual sovereignty producing for the manipulators. It also keeps them from taking any action toward regaining their individual sovereignty. They fail to realize that, among themselves, money is a drug-sedative that mass manipulators are happy for competent, aggressive, highly productive, individual sovereignty people to have. It keeps them passive. The wealthy and passive thereby join the "lower classes" that the priests persuaded to accept money as payment for the wrong done them. The only difference is the amount of money needed to buy their honor.

In the world of international commerce, a very important thing about money is this: Money is the power of a government that can be given into the hands of anonymous persons. It can be given into the hands of the enemies of the government. History shows what can happen when this is done.

Along with word control, money collected from the people was a major tool the Catholic Church used to take control within the Roman Empire. Money was the power of the Roman Empire, itself. The Roman Empire's own money, injected into the combination of words and force used by the Church, worked so successfully that, in the end, kings held their "position" because a pope placed a crown on their heads.

Then, as kings revolted against control by the Catholic Church, the struggle for power between mass manipulators became more complex. Anonymous individuals began to use the government's power that was packaged up in money. An international organization of Jewish bankers, recognizing that money is the power of governments that can be given into the hands of anonymous persons, began to manipulate the governments themselves.

The demonstrated fact that a group-entity other than the openly recognized government - a church or an organization of bankers - could use the government's own money to destroy the government, itself, became impressive. Some of the individual sovereignty people, who had seen their culture destroyed by the clever priests, tried their hands at using money as a weapon. They tried to form "honorable" group-entities and use money to protect them from group-entities that obviously promoted the culture of mass manipulation.

Wiser ones recognized that opposing cultures cannot be mixed. They recognized the necessity for segregating themselves. They sought out areas where they could hope to continue the defense of the individual sovereignty culture that had bred them.

THE REVOLT OF THE VIKINGS

Opposing cultures cannot be mixed. The opposition between them is mortal and eternal. The culture of mass manipulation drove the last remnant of the individual sovereignty people, who had avoided involvement, into hideouts along the northern coasts.

Denmark, Norway, and Sweden afforded the best areas for their resistance. They took to the sea in long boats from inlets (inlet = Vik) and were called Vikings.

Within the confused chaos that was now Northern Europe, the Vikings recognized that their major enemy was the Catholic Church. It was the underhanded tactics of the Church, not the open force of the Roman Empire, that had done such vast damage to their culture.

Beginning about fifteen hundred years ago they went every place that was available to their long black boats with about forty men each. They launched raids in areas where the Church dominated the people. With indignation and contempt they killed those who had been faithless to themselves and their own culture and accepted the enemy. They, of course, made a special point of burning the monasteries and nunneries and killing monks, nuns, and priests.

They freed great areas in England and Northern France (Normandy) from Church control. They went as far as Greenland and America searching for new homelands.

They were making a valiant stand in defense of their culture. They were already badly outnumbered. But they were strong-willed, steadfast in their comradeship, and of unexcelled courage when facing their enemies.

They held out for about six hundred years. But gradually, one leader after another met some kindly priest, who was sincerely struggling for a buried truth about Jesus underneath the falseness of the manipulators. One leader after another glimpsed what the sincere priests were seeking. They allowed the anti-Christ "Christianity" to come in.

Then priests, nuns, and monks were allowed to teach little children the twisted words of the Church.

Rollo set up a Viking power in Normandy strong enough to continually raid Paris, but he joined the Church and was accepted as part of the overall power in 912. He was given a "position" with the title of Duke.

Gorm set up a protected individual sovereignty area encompassing all Denmark which lasted until his death in 940. Then his son, Harold Bluetooth, was baptized and allowed the Church to take over in Denmark.

Harold the Fairhaired consolidated all Norway into resistance against the Church in 872. His great-grandson let in the power of the Church in 1020.

Sweden held out for almost another hundred years but finally lost the battle against the mass manipulators.

The children were then all sent to schools where they were taught nothing about the all important conflict of cultures. Instead, they were taught that their ancestors were "barbarians" and the "fortunate" children would now have the great priviledge of building a "modern civilized" group-entity.

The Church's practices of selectively breeding for mass manipulation were rapidly put into effect. But the products of a culture that had long been breeding in the opposite direction did not provide much base for selective breeding in a diametrically opposed direction.

Also, fragments of the old cultural practices persisted.

* * *

Aside from the flesh and blood individual sovereignty people who came from countless centuries of selective breeding by their culture, and aside from the disjointed fragments of the old cultural practices that have persisted, the thing about the Western World that distinguishes it from the Orient is the memory that the culture of mass manipulation does not have to be accepted as "the way things are."

In the Western World, there is still a cherished knowledge that once a fully functioning culture of individual sovereignty existed. And it is well remembered that such a culture made for a life enriched – beyond the conception of manipulated masses – by deep abiding love and joyful comradeship.

For more millenniums than there exists any historical record, that culture was maintained against the encroaching culture of mass manipulation.

That memory has not yet been fully destroyed.

SEGREGATION PROVIDES A NEW OPPORTUNIIY

About four hundred years ago, people who had been deprived of their individual sovereignty in Europe began coming to America where the population was so sparce that individuals could hope to make a new life.

Recovery of their heritage was not easy. The ways of mass manipulators had been imposed on them for almost a thousand years. Because the force-backed brainwashing had been so intense in Europe - with torture, imprisonment and conspicuous public death for all who said, or were suspected of thinking, anything not approved by the priests - many of the colonies merely became imitations of what was going on in Europe. Some had word-contollers acting like "little popes" and trying to set up the sort of theocracy that the people had been brainwashed to call "religion."

But living close to Nature gradually restored perception to some extent. Also, some individuals among the people retained a knowledge of their individual sovereignty heritage.

About three hundred years ago, some of the people, led by Roger Williams, began actively to oppose theocracy - the form of government that tries to hide the underhanded force behind it and pretends to be a freely accepted "religion."

About two hundred years ago, the Americans began actively to oppose domination by group-entities in Europe.

Those who had a clear picture of what had happened to them in Europe knew that they could not fully restore their original culture all at once. The culture of mass manipulation had been imposed on them in carefully measured steps, and the way back to their own culture would need to be in carefully measured steps. However they had thrown off enough of the brainwashing forced on them to make a start.

A group of people in thirteen colonies decided to try forming a government of sovereign individuals as the

Greeks had tried to do. In their Declaration of Independence, written by Thomas Jefferson, they proclaimed themselves independent of all group-entities, declared that Nature and Nature's God had clearly made all individuals equally sovereign, and declared that any laws enforced by group action could only be made by the individuals who composed the group.

The people of the United States had to fight to enforce their segregation from the group-entities of Europe. They won the fight and established a Constitution making individual sovereignty, as set forth in the Declaration of Independence, into a written Constitution that outlined the government's functions.

The Constitution set austere limits on the Government's power. The people wanted to restore the culture that was their heritage.

Because of the segregation that an ocean provided at that time, the people of the United States were able to make great progress toward forming a government that would implement their recaptured culture. Their success in doing this became conspicuous. America became known as the land of opportunity for those who did not like what had happened to them in Europe and wanted to make a new start.

For almost one hundred and fifty years the people of the United States made spectacular strides toward recapturing their individual sovereignty. The people could continually "go west" - could segregate themselves from any control by those trying to move the new Government toward mass manipulation. As open territory after open territory was settled, the recovering people were becoming stronger in their resistance to manipulation.

But the culture of mass manipulation is a difficult thing to be rid of after it has once been imposed on a people. Brainwashing for mass manipulation had been very effective on some who came along with those wanting to escape it. And others, who consciously wanted the culture of mass manipulation, infiltrated and added their conscious will to the direction that the Catholic Church had forcefully imposed on the brainwashed.

The culture of mass manipulation is an accretion of

implements and ways of using those implements that has been built up over more than six thousand years. Those who consciously want the culture preserve and add to the accretion, while carefully dressing it up in a masquerade called "civilization."

The primitive form of mass manipulation was simply a word controlled gang killing off those who would not willingly submit to the manipulated group's domination.

The next form was adding the "carrots" produced by enforced organization to the "stick" of open force - and hiding open force under the tricky mask of money.

The form that had been effective against the Northern Europeans was that which depended on gradual infiltration of individuals who lulled the people into dropping their defenses by a pretense of good will - while the infiltrators gained enough strength to deceitfully manipulate their unsuspecting hosts. This was the form that began to have its effect in the United States.

The system of "pork barrel politics" began to line up greedy groups behind politicians who were clever at making underhanded "cloakroom" deals - and dressing them up in deceitful oratory when presenting them in congressional sessions open to the public.

As this system became more widespread, government by underhanded conspiracies between politicians was accepted in Congress as the most effective way to "get things done." It soon became virtually impossible for an honest representative of the people to oppose it. He was shunned as naive and useless by the old hands.

At some unknown time a "cloakroom" conspiracy that directly opposed the Constitutional Government was formed. The "cloakroom" conspiracy showed its undercover existence - and its commitment to the mass manipulation from which the people of the United States were trying to escape - on December 23, 1913.

On December 23, 1913 the underhanded conspiracy gave unmistakable evidence that it was out to destroy the Constitutional Government. It began to take control.

On December 23, 1913 there were enough elected members of Congress who were either unbelievably naive or willing to destroy the Constitutional Government to pass the Federal Reserve Act.

This Act was in direct violation of Article 1, Section 8 of the United States Constitution. Article 1, Section 8 gave Congress the power – and obligation – to regulate the value of money. That, of course, meant to regulate the value of money by laws the people could see.

The Federal Reserve Act delegated the power to regulate the value of money to non-elected persons who could make undercover agreements with greedy groups within the United States and with foreign governments – and the voting public would be helpless to control them. This "cloakroom" deal could have no purpose but to give a major weapon into the hands of manipulators who opposed the Constitution – and to hide the use made of that weapon from the people.

A unit of money is a unit of force that belongs to the force-controller whose stamp is on the money. Money is the power of a government that can be given into the hands of anonymous persons. It can be given into the hands of the enemy of the government. The power to regulate the value of United States money is not less than the power to regulate the military might of the United States.

The Federal Reserve Act gave future "cloakroom" deals power to manipulate the domestic economy – and to manipulate the power of the United States Government relative to other governments.

Such an unconstitutional act was possible only because the people had been brainwashed to believe that the economy obeys natural laws of supply and demand and money is merely "a medium of exchange."

The "cloakroom" conspiracy obviously included, and continues to include as its major strategy planners, some who have a will for, a long heritage of, and an expertise in the deceitful form of mass manipulation. Exercise of the undercover power has been restrained and carefully camouflaged.

A twisted use of money rivals a twisted use of words as a tool for brainwashing and mass manipulation.

Money that is not going to be used exclusively as an underhanded tool of manipulators, money that can be used by individuals as an honest medium of exchange, must have intrinsic value. That value must be known to the people.

Also the commodity that gives value to the money must be something wanted by the people. The function of a government that is dedicated to the welfare of the people is to ensure that the amount of the commodity is what is stated on the face of the money – and that the money can readily be exchanged for the stated commodity.

Whether coined gold, coined silver, a square foot of living space, a daily ration of food as established for the armed service, a bushel of wheat, or something else is used to give intrinsic value to the money is not the most significant point to be settled.

In the United States, it is the constitutional obligation of Congress to regulate the value of U. S. money – by legislation that is known to the people. The people can then see what is happening and do what needs to be done for their self-protection.

If, for example, oil, or certain minerals that are more abundant in other places than in the United States were made the basis for the value for U. S. money by Congress, it would immediately be apparent to the U. S. people that Congress, as a body, had committed an act of treason. It would be obvious that Congress had conspired to weaken the United States and make it vulnerable to attack.

Then, if "government by the people" was a functioning reality, the people would arrest Congress as a body and try each individual for treason.

The present unconstitutional control of U. S. money by the Federal Reserve System has continued only because the "cloakroom" deals have hidden what was happening from the people.

Nothing – absolutely nothing – now backs U. S. money but force – the consolidated economic and military force of the United States.

Money – that is backed by no commodity of intrinsic value to an individual – can have its value manipulated so completely that it gives the manipulators full contol over the domestic economy. And the non-elected members of the Federal Reserve System have been given this unconstitutional power to manipulate the value of U. S. money.

In international relations, the value of U. S. money can now be secretly manipulated relative to the value of a foreign government's money to improve that foreign economy or completely destroy it. In international relations, the act of regulating money - especially the money of a government as powerful as the United States whose money is backed by nothing but force - can only be construed as making an undercover alliance, or provoking an act of war. And the non-elected members of the Federal Reserve System have been given this undercover power to make secret alliances and provoke war. The Congress, the President, and the people of the United States are then subjected to the conditions that the undercover manipulators create.

The United States as a nation was betrayed by those who passed the Federal Reserve Act, and every individual in the United States was enslaved to undercover manipulators by that act.

How can a U. S. citizen exchange his money for the commodity that gives it value - when that commodity is control of the United State's total force by undercover manipulators?

He cannot readily do so. He can only make efforts in that direction that to many appear shameful. He can contribute to a "legal" lobby that attempts to use money to manipulate members of Congress to vote for certain "laws." The lobby may be successful if the "laws" are petty ones that do not conflict with the manipulators' overall strategy. Or as an individual he can try making undercover bribes to law makers or law enforcers. There is no other way that a U. S. citizen can "cash in" his money when there is nothing backing it but the manipulated undercover use of pseudo-legal force.

What about the international field where the force is the undercover manipulated force of the U. S. as a whole?

Other governments can make "cloakroom" deals with the manipulators of U. S. money to have their own money (their own power) increased in relation to the money of the

United States. And this is all done by the undercover manipulators to whom Congress betrayed the American people on December 23, 1913. All the people see are the wars that occur when the foreign governments refuse to bend to the will of the undercover manipulators.

Every day the current Congress is in session and fails to repeal the Federal Reserve Act, it ratifies the treasonous betrayal of the United States people that took place on December 23, 1913.

There are many individuals in the United States who are fully aware of this condition. Why is it not brought to public attention so that the people can demand that it be corrected?

This is prevented by a series of other unconstitutional Congressional actions that began in 1924.

Radio had been invented. Because waves carrying electrical impulses are limited, there would be total chaos if their use were not regulated. The invention of radio required that the use of the air waves be considered in context with the constitutional prohibition on Congress against making laws interfering with freedom of speech. The invention of radio obviously required action. But the First Amendment to the Constitution prohibited any action by Congress. The action required was an update of the First Amendment, made by due process of law, to deal with the new medium affecting free speech – because the existing First Amendment specifically forbid Congress to do what it did.

Congress defied the Constitution. Congress made "cloakroom" deals and followed them up with unconstitutional "laws" designating radio stations as commercial enterprises to be licensed by obsure agencies. These "cloakroom" deals obviously paved the way for the licensing agencies to be controlled by future "cloakroom" deals. This provided mass manipulators, licensed as station owners, with a power of censorship denied to the United States Government, itself. The internal, undercover enemy was thereby given greater power than the Constitutional Government.

When television was invented, the unconstitutional "laws" already on the record were extended to this far more effective medium.

No matter who, even the greatest patriot, might be licensed to make radio or television broadcasts under present "laws," the licensing and the broadcast would be unconstitutional. And it is certain that patriots are not the ones that the manipulators have licensed. It is glaringly conspicuous that the mass manipulators who are now actually in control of U. S. television are opposed to the culture of individual sovereignty and to the Constitutional United States Government – the only implement of individual sovereignty that is still theoretically operative in the world today.

This censorship by an enemy of the United States Government over what the people hear and see amounts to control over Congress and over the President of the United States. The control now exercised by these – never publicly recognized – internal enemies is as complete as if they were an armed enemy with an occupying army.

Every attempt made by the people to "peaceably assemble and petition" for restoration of Constitutional Government has been branded "subversive" by those in control of television – and they have managed to manipulate ways of silencing opposition to what they are doing.

The undercover manipulators in control of television now so completely dominate the press that major newspapers cannot survive if they oppose them. Because they control television, the manipulators even control book distribution, and book selection for libraries.

The de facto government of the United States – the undercover one that manipulates the puppet Constitutional Government by control of money and television – is, to everyone but the United States citizens who are constantly bombarded with the manipulators' propaganda, the most conspicuous culture of mass manipulation that exists in the world today.

As compared to mass manipulation cultures throughout history, this one is a new form of unprecedented virulence. It has taken over without its take-over being seen by the manipulated. And yet, its diametrical opposition to the Constitutional Government, to the ideals of those who founded the United States, to all human reason, to natural evolution, and to Nature's God, is shamelessly glaring.

Because it has a more varied base to work on, the planned selective breeding now taking place in the United States is far more effective than that of the European inquisitions of the middle ages.

Those bred by and having a heritage of the individual sovereignty culture are so frustrated by living under a culture of mass manipulation that they account for less than zero population growth. Almost no individuals who were bred by the culture of individual sovereignty now choose to immigrate and become United States citizens. Meanwhile the de facto government brings in, or allows to come in illegally, those it can manipulate. Also the "laws" that it pressures the puppet government to make encourage prolific breeding of the incompetent and unperceptive who can be manipulated.

All history has shown that opposing cultures cannot be mixed. But this is the most impressive example of that fact ever known. Never before has a mortal enemy taken over a people's government without their knowledge.

The United States - which was founded by those bred for and trying to reclaim their culture of individual sovereignty - is now undergoing the most rapid human culture of humans for mass manipulation ever known in the whole history of the human species.

THE CURRENT WORLDWIDE PICTURE

Since the United States ceased to function as its Constitution prescribed, there exists no place on earth where the culture of individual sovereignty is now implemented by a recognizable government power.

If we look only at "the way things are" it would appear that the culture of individual sovereignty has failed – and the human species is doomed to regression or extinction.

There is more reason for hope if we look at the human products of three billion years of evolution who continue to resist the culture of mass manipulation.

We recognize that less than a fifth of the present world's population was bred by the individual sovereignty culture. However the desire for individual sovereignty exists in many individuals throughout the world who have no history of the culture. They may not even recognize that any human culture of humans has ever been practiced. Without reference to any cultural heritage, they merely think of themselves as having been strong enough to resist mass manipulation. They see individual sovereignty as an innate urge, they see it as being the nature of humans – even as it is the nature of other living things. They simply think that Nature has been perverted by mass manipulators. They would welcome the opportunity to participate in any feasible action to eliminate the practices of the manipulators.

All of us who perceive the significance of our individual sovereignty cultural heritage recognize that the entire human species is now being bred for such complete lack of perception, and such complete acceptence of group-entities as "the way things are," that it appears to be passing the point of no return.

Both the Oriental and the Western systems have become fully effective, full blown human cultures of humans. Both now selectively breed for zombis that can be manipulated.

The control of the people within the areas dominated by each system is now complete. Now the focus is on which system can demonstrate its "superiority" by extending its area of control.

Both have now adopted the same language for use in combination with force. Both use modern meaningless word replacements for "destroying the wicked and the evildoers that the strong harm not the weak." In the Western system, the war cry is "our democracy against communism." In the Oriental system the war cry is "our democracy against capitalistic imperialism." "Demoncracy," in both systems, is merely an illusion that the manipulated people are still individuals making their own choices. This illusion is maintained by herding them to polling booths where they cast votes for one of the tweedle-dee tweedle-dum choices that the manipulators allow them make.

What is the real difference between the current systems of mass manipulation that the manipulators are now pitting against each other?

Because mass manipulators in the Western World have had six thousand years of using carrots along with the stick, and because they have been able to enslave and use the abilities of a people bred for individual sovereignty, the "standard of living" has been higher in the West.

However the basic difference is this:

In the Orient, mass force is seen for what it is.

In the West, mass force was originally camouflaged as "the will of god." Now those Western manipulators who have a heritage of conquest by deceit are intoxicated with their demonstrated success in camouflaging raw force under the cover of money.

This undercover use of force makes it possible for them to continue the same language of twisted words about "thou shalt not kill" that originally confused and led the individual sovereignty people to kill off each other. Destroying those who are consciously committed to the culture of individual sovereignty is their major objective. World Wars I and II, into which they manipulated the individual sovereignty people, did much to accomplish this. The use they make of money, television, and compulsory "education" is clear evidence that they want to continue manipulating individual sovereignty people to fight and kill other individual sovereignty people until all who oppose mass manipulation have been bred out of the human species.

Never in history has open, recognizable force destroyed a functioning culture of individual sovereignty. As described in the Siegfried legend, those committed to this culture are vulnerable only at a spot on their backs not touched by the dragon's blood in which they bathed. Their comradeship and love, born of their relationships exclusively with each other, leave them vulnerable to an enemy who has not declared himself as such – and who bears no visible weapon.

Originally the individual sovereignty people were under pressure from two sides. But they never fell before mass force. They demonstrated to the whole world that sovereign individuals can effectively resist open, recognizable force.

Their culture remained fully functional east of the Rhine and north of the Danube Rivers – even while the Romans set against their borders at least half of all the legions they could muster within the most formidable empire of manipulated masses the West had ever known. The culture of individual sovereignty, which always expands rapidly under conditions favoring individual perception and an open appeal to reason, was never overcome by force that was open and honest. Only an undefended area where the individual sovereignty people could be knifed in the back has made possible what has happened.

The original Northern European individual sovereignty society fell to lies and deceit of enemies who were eager to show that their hands were empty of recognizable weapons.

The same pattern was evident when the people of the United States, unconquered by the force of a recognizable and declared enemy, fell before mass manipulators who falsified their allegiance to the Constitutional Government and took control as deceitful infiltrators building a network that bored from within.

When considering strategy, it is therefore fitting that we focus our view of current conditions on the mass manipulators whose own strategy of battle relies on infiltration, lies, and deceit that provoke others to fight among themselves while they, the actual enemies, carry no visible weapons. Because, more than those of the opposing culture, we have bred the capacity for comradeship and love to an extremely high degree, we are slow to recognize that an enemy "can smile and smile and be a villian still."

If the culture of mass manipulation passes the point of no return, it will make little difference whether it was the one that had its origin in the Orient or in the West. The only real advantage of now being in the West is that there are some of us who remember and cherish our heritage of being bred by a successful, functioning, adequately defended culture of individual sovereignty. We know our aspirations are not the dreams of an impractical utopia. We know a culture of individual sovereignty can work and if it were worldwide there would be no more mass warfare.

Even in the middle of manipulated mass madness, we retain some measure of our innate perception. We know that our culture was Nature's way. In Nature, we know that we have an ally that will continue the ideals and direction to which we are committed – even if it requires replacing the whole human species with another form of life.

Our sanity, as we view all the manipulated forces that stand against us, requires conscious and continuous awareness that "Nature and Nature's God" are here to stay. Evolution, the method of Nature that created us, is here to stay. The human species continues from the plateau of sexual beings, with a sex based perception, or it regresses and its individuals become parts of an asexual group-entity.

If an asexual "will to power" is used to create group-entities, then mass warfare – with the most effective weapons human ingenuity can devise – is inevitable. But this replacement of sovereign individuals with group-entities will not be "victory over nature." The human species will be replaced by a species more fitted to do what the individual sovereignty people tried so valiantly to accomplish.

What can be the nature of the manipulators that are now pushing the human species back toward the way of life passed by evolving living things more than six hundred million years ago?

If we want to be generous, we can assume that the mass manipulators lack knowledge regarding the overall effect of their actions. We can assume that they have merely become involved in a game and think there is a prize called "a position of power." We can assume that they do not know how greatly they are degrading and destroying the quality of life when they present sex as nothing more than a source of sensual enjoyment – as eating food is to an asexual animal. We can assume that they don't know what is happening to innate creative perception when life is presented as a game of acquiring the assembly line products of "civilization." We can assume they do not recognize that "achieving a position of power" within a group–entity is becoming a part of an organism that evolution surpassed six hundred million years ago – the asexual entity.

Perhaps we make a mistake if we seek to be generous and regard the manipulators as "decent human beings who are just stupid." Perhaps the monstrosity of what they are doing is too great for us to believe that it comes from human will.

True, the total monstrosity is a cultural accretion of individual human wills – but those who carry it on are constantly adding to it. As individuals they may "smile and smile," and thereby tempt us to accept them as harmless, but it is by their fruits that we must know them. The fruits of what they have done and are doing show a superficial cleverness that proclaims their objective of "victory over nature" is not set forth with total ignorance of that objective's scope and monstrosity. They have concentrated on Nature's obstacle to what they are doing – sex.

Centuries ago the manipulators successfully used sexual relations to enhance the "authority" of the group entity over individuals. They encouraged the manipulated masses to stone to death anyone who did not submit to the group's "right" to "authorize" sexual relations.

When the manipulated group ceased to stone to death those who showed no respect for the group–entity's arrogated "right" to "authorize" individual sexual relations, the manipulators began to destroy respect for sex, itself. They actively promoted homosexuality and perversion.

In their attempts to present sex as nothing more than a source of sensual enjoyment, as eating food is to an asexual animal, they promoted the misuse of the very word "sex." In current use it has been changed to mean "sexual relations."

That leaves no word for a development that has been the major focus of evolution for six hundred million years of trial and error.

Sex is not "sexual relations." Sex is a plateau of evolution that needs to be seen as such. The ecstasy and subtle perception, that selective evolution has at last woven into sexual beings, leads one to the joyful perception of the direction and wonder of Nature that works underneath consciousness in all living things.

Because the plateau of sex evolved delicate perception, humans began to consciously recognize that wonder underneath consciousness at work wherever they saw it manifest in Nature. They perceived it within themselves and without. They saw it in the light. They saw it in the darkness. Each small human could thrill to the tallness of a pine tree, relax one's being into the fragrance of a rose, expand with joy before the glorious color of a sunrise, and weep before the beauty of the stars. Then, at last, each small conscious human began to glimpse the awe-inspiring privilege of his place as a direct interacting part of the grand totality.

The manipulators appear to clearly recognize that the perception arising from leaving sexual discrimination where Nature placed it – in the conscious-subconscious thoughts of the individual – is something that must be destroyed one way or another. Their history-old objective is monstrous beyond acceptance by anyone we can consider a sane person. But although, instead of being locked in insane asylums, they smile and profess beneficent objectives, we can still recognize the psychotic suicidal maliciousness that wills: "If we cannot have our 'positions of power' we will drag the entire human species into the pit with us rather than admit our falsity."

Some of us see with painful clearness the march of madness over individual sovereignty that is upheld, by those who mouth phrases supplied by the manipulators, as "the triumph of civilization over barbarism."

Most painful of the things we now watch, in line with the manipulated objective of "victory over nature," is the selective breeding for lack of perception so that massed humans can be more easily manipulated.

While the selective breeding is still incomplete, while

all perception has not yet been entirely bred out, the view of another spectacle causes us pain. The continuing culture of mass manipulation requires that even the remaining vestige of perception be made non-functional by brainwashing. The methods vary but susceptibility to manipulation is always the goal that the manipulators seek to "achieve."

The original Oriental form of brainwashing was expressed by Laotze, founder of Taoism, about twenty-six hundred years ago in these words: "The sage, in the exercise of government, empties the people's minds, fills their bellies, weakens their wills, strengthens their bones. He constantly tries to keep them without knowledge and without desire, and where there are those who have knowledge, to keep them from presuming to act on it. Where there is this abstinence from action, good order is universal."

The original Western form of brainwashing was to fill the people's minds so full of lies about man-invented gods that any remaining perception of those bred for lack of perception was overruled with words.

The present method in the West is "education" and entertainment – the attempt to fill minds so full of inconsequential pap passing for information that the manipulated cannot sweep it away and view themselves and their relation to the world in anything approaching clear perspective. Red herrings are dragged across every significant thought by manipulators before it reaches consideration by the media-controlled public.

For instance: The major concern of most people today is mass warfare and the impressive weapons that have been created for that purpose. Several writers, popular enough to be interviewed on televison, have made the point that, of all the millions of species of life known to science, only humans and the "social" insects engage in mass warfare. This observed fact is crowded out by a flood of other factual information – before the profound significance of it can be perceived.

The two forms of brainwashing – emptying people's minds, or filling them so full that there is no room for their innate perception to surface – appear equally effective as methods for mass manipulation. Both systems result in preventing the individual from relating objective perception to the aboriginal creative consciousness within – as a basis for viewing total reality in clear perspective. Direct relationship between the individual and total reality must be destroyed before the individual can accept relationship with the group-entity as having top priority. Which system can give worldwide control by most effectively "accomplishing" this is the only concern of the manipulators who now pit against each other the Oriental and Western systems of brainwashing.

* * *

What opinion might we expect of the current problem of humans on earth if we imagined ourselves viewed by a "more advanced" people on another planet, or by a people of another dimension living among us, or simply by some among us who have allowed the perspective of the aboriginal creative intelligence to permeate their beings? Imagine what they would say:

Objective observer: "Three billion years of evolution has produced humans as a species of the most promising potential to be found anywhere in the universe. In the regressive insects they have before them the clear picture of what will happen to them if they continue their present direction. And still they continue."

Concerned observer: "I don't like the destiny that looms before them. Can't they see that destiny as it is set out before them in the world of reality - in the living language of the aboriginal creative consciousness?"

Objective observer: "They see in a clouded detached fashion without making a connection between what they see and what they are doing. Their minds are too full of garbage to see anything clearly. They obviously know that they are opposing natural evolution. But in World War II they killed off fifty million of their fittest young men - even while seeking ways to preserve the deformed and incompetent. They call human life sacred and profane its quality in order to preserve no more than a beating heart and some semblance of food digestion. They see the termite female turned into an egg laying factory, a helpless thing several hundred times the size of an ordinary termite, attended by de-sexed individuals who make "test-tube" modifications to produce the functional types needed by the group-entity - and they find it repulsive. But one of their entertainment producers, Aldous Huxley, describes the same condition as being that toward which the human species is rapidly moving. With a supercilious smile he titles the description "Brave New World" and they merely find the picture amusing. They fail to see that they, themselves, have been going through the termite, and the "Brave New World," de-sexing process throughout all the history of their mass manipulation culture. That culture has bred such lack of perception that they reject reality and choose the titillation of drugs or word-confused thought."

Concerned observer: "Potentially they are a very fine species; it is even difficult to imagine how the best of them could be more fittingly developed toward becoming diverse interacting facets of the aboriginal creative intelligence. Can you visualize no destiny for them in the extant design of being but for the whole species to become extinct by group-entity fighting group-entity with the powerful weapons of mass warfare they have invented?"

Objective observer: "Enough of them could survive total warfare to continue the species but whether its continuation would be worthwhile is problematical. They have been so completely conditioned to think that group-entities are essential to survival that they would probably repeat their history all over again."

Concerned observer: "I hate to think of them becoming extinct. But that, I admit, would be preferable to their success in the direction they are going - recreating the asexual group-entity after the fashion of the insects. I'd like to think that the present total world domination of the mass manipulation culture could act as a fire that burned out the dross - and those who survived the experience would be so strengthed that they could never again be manipulated, and would be too wise to try to manipulate others."

Objective observer: "That well might happen, if you are not contemplating a unique accident by which a devastating atomic war would somehow preserve selected individuals. Individual will is the direction determining essence of, and reason for, all living things. Those who lack the perception to reject the culture of mass manipulation are dross that are better drained from the stream of evolution. Only those who throw the full weight of their force, or will, for individual integrity are fit brands for a continuing life segregated from the burning."

ABOUT THE BOOK'S AUTHORS,
the
VALORIAN SOCIETY

The Valorian Society is a non-profit corporation for the purpose of public education. The corporation organizes the study, preparation, and distribution of varied informative, literary, and art works, along with specific works for adult discussion groups, and child education.

The Society is oriented on the culture of individual sovereignty. Some members were already committed to a "dress rehearsal for the culture of individual sovereignty" before the corporation was formed. These members have provided much of the driving force and creative work behind the Society's accomplishments.

The "dress rehearsal" is a day to day way of life different from that enforced on everyone in the culture of mass manipulation. This day to day simulated individual sovereignty provides concrete examples to children of interpersonal relationships that are more in harmony with their innate impulses than what they could see, and hear advocated, in the world of manipulated masses. Such examples form a conspicuous contrast to present conditions in the outside world. The contrast stimulates perceptive thought, leads to intelligent questions, and provides a basis for explaining to children how people developed the - presently worldwide - mass madness that is the problem of the human species.

"Dress rehearsal" is the nearest approach to a culture of individual sovereignty that can now be practiced - even in the Western "free world." The Constitution established the United States as a government to defend sovereign individuals from group-entities promoting the culture of mass manipulation, but it no longer functions in this respect. The enemies of individual sovereignty within the United States began their first unmistakable attempt to destroy the United States Government about seventy years ago, as detailed in our work "Human History." They pressured Congress into making "laws" exceeding its Constitutional authority. These "laws" funneled power into the hands of the manipulators and enabled them to use that power without the public becoming aware of what was happening. These internal enemies of the United States now have as much control as if they had full support from an occupying army.

The manipulators who have this control over the United States are committed to the culture that is in mortal opposition to the individual sovereignty culture. They want no public awareness that the culture they are trying to destroy exists or ever did exist. They do not want a "dress rehearsal" example. They do not want any awareness of cultural conflict injected into their manipulative "education" of children. And they do not want public awareness of the cultural conflict stimulated by open public adult discussions.

The Valorian Society and all those engaged in the associated "dress rehearsal" fully support and conform to the Constitutional laws of the United States. Believing that confrontation on any point less than the total issue plays into the enemy's hands, we also conform to all the unconstitutional "laws" that Congress has been pressured to put on record.

Because the Valorian Society is legally incorporated as a non-profit educational society, and its recorded purpose of public education requires free speech and free press, the unconstitutional "laws" that provide a method for censorship by an enemy controlling the United States are extremely irksome. However, our strategy is to obey even the inch-by-inch "laws" that chip away at the world's last government committed to individual sovereignty – until the Constitutional Government can be fully restored.

Because the controlling enemy does not yet feel confident to openly challenge the Constitution of the United States as a whole, we sovereign individuals who live in the United States and fully support the Constitution have only one formidable problem. It is a problem that we share with sovereign individuals throughout the world. This shared problem stimulates our empathy for those in areas where the ones committed to mass manipulation are already the official government.

Since the United States fell under control of its enemies, there is nowhere in the world where sovereign individuals are not simply prisoners of a single "one world" enemy. The whole world has become one planetary prison camp run by those committed to the culture of mass manipulation.

This anti-Nature, anti-reason condition is so ridiculous that passive acceptance of it would insult our intelligence. Can a clear look at the facts fail to insult the intelligence of any person with perception? The facts are so few and simple that the ridiculousness of the condition should be glaringly conspicuous.

The culture of mass manipulation has been selectively breeding humans who would accept life as mere units of a controlled group-entity for perhaps 15,000 years. However, this is only 1/40,000th of the time that natural selection bred all living things for perceptive awareness of their individual sovereignty. The humans who retain the conscious will to individual sovereignty doubtless still account for well over half the world population. And those who are consciously committed to the culture of mass manipulation, even under governments that openly advocate communism, almost certainly amount to less than ten percent of those over whom they exercise control. Even if we ignore the zombis that the culture of mass manipulation has already selectively bred, the control of individual sovereigns by less than one fifth their number of mass manipulators is too ridiculous for passive acceptance.

But such control is an undeniable current fact that must be admitted before considering what can be done about it.

The first problem that we, who are committed sovereign individuals, must face is the problem that always faces prisoners - communication with each other, when those who hold them prisoners live in constant fear that communication will lead to cooperative action.

The fact that we sovereign individuals - particularly when we live in the "free" Western World - have the communication problem typical of prisoners is a seemingly ridiculous thing to admit – even when the undeniable fact is constantly before us.

Most of us move about freely and talk freely. The present restraint on communication is something different from that known in conventional prison camps. We are not only permitted to talk. We are prompted and encouraged to talk. This total reversal camouflages the fact that ours is the age-old problem of prisoners.

Instead of the conventionally enforced silence, the enemy's current method of stopping communication is based on confusion. We are permitted and encouraged to say anything that creates or adds to the confused babble. The censorship consists not of stopping talk but of twisting or drowning out anything significant that is said.

If sovereign individual prisoners say anything significant, the manipulators controlling the media will twist it if they can, and drown it out if they cannot twist it into something that, by unreasoned association, implies discredit on individual sovereignty or those advocating it. Insignifcant babble, used to create confusion and swallow up anything significant, is a weapon used in connection with the controlled media to accomplish this unique form of super-censorship.

In most areas of the worldwide prison, individuals can talk. But selection of what will actually be heard by a sizeable public is under control of those committed to the culture of mass manipulation.

In the United States, the Constitution prohibits the Constitutional Government from abridging freedom of speech. But the manipulators who have a control of the media denied to the Government are not the Constitutional Government. They would merely laugh at any petition for a redress of grievances. They see the U. S. Government as being nothing but their puppet. They think of themselves as being above the Government.

The Valorian Society recognizes the stated condition but does not accept it passively. For over fifteen years we have created and distributed brochures and books on the various aspects of our worldwide problem that add up to significant communication. The active response and rapid extension of communication lines has been extremely gratifying.

Also, we have discovered that, in the United States, where the manipulators are not yet quite ready to challenge the Constitution as a whole, we can simulate a desirable life as sovereign individuals - if we refuse to be taken in by the efforts our enemies make to give our "dress rehearsal" some "well deserved publicity" - their kind. We encourage others to follow our example.

Those who are consciously committed to the culture of individual sovereignty, and have sufficient friends so committed to provide a social group of a size that all find satisfactory, can find simulation of individual sovereignty highly rewarding. The social group may consist of only two persons, a single family, or a fairly large number of individuals held together socially, economically and/or by location. The location may be within a city, in a secluded rural area, or anywhere. In the United States there are a variety of legal forms that such a group can use to enhance its functional efficacy. In many other countries the difficulties are greater. But, even so, a "dress rehearsal" for individual sovereignty is worth a substantial risk.

John Harland's book, "Brave New World, A Different Projection," describes a small self-sustaining "dress rehearsal" group in an isolated valley that has very limited contact with the outside world. Jill von Konen's "Camp 38" is a fictional projection of an inconspicuous group of substantial size that is dedicated to a fully functioning culture of individual sovereignty. Both writers are members of the Valorian Society.

All members of the Valorian Society have found that separation between a simulated world of individual sovereignty and the world controlled by the mass manipulators helps us keep the problem in focus. The central core of the Valorian Society is continuing a "dress rehearsal" segregation as an aid to further refinement of communication materials. There is still much to be done by us and by others who are also working at the same task. The soundest of materials are essential when we move into the public arena, where the enemy's stategy of battle is "confuse the issue."

In cooperation with the American Christian Church and the Perceptive Baptist Church, the Valorian Society sponsors the Individual Sovereignty Society. The ISS is actively implementing a specific, precisely set forth, strategy for restoring Constitutional Government in the United States.

A member of the Valorian Society, Erik Holden, wrote the incisive comments bound with the "American Christian Bible," by Thomas Jefferson. This is the edition of the so-called Jefferson Bible that is used by the American Christian Church and the Perceptive Baptist Church. These churches are primarily concerned with turning the stampede of the anti-Christ "Christians," who have played into the hands of the mass manipulators. Those who are aware of the harm being done by the good intentions ot these anti-Christ "Christians," and who have a basis of empathy with them, may find this a fertile field for active work.

There is an enormous open field for public presentation – to a live audience – of fully organized ideas that would turn the stampede of those brainwashed to accept the manipulators' propaganda that they call "the consensus of scientific opinion."

We have found that open discussions focusing on a specific significant written work – and kept in focus by host-leaders who ask questions without making comments – can be very effective. They do more than merely stimulate public thought. They also enable perceptive persons to distinguish between enemies, zombies, and potential friends. By doing this they provide a basis for forming desirable relationships. The Valorian Society makes plans and provides materials for such discussions.

The preparation of books and materials for sound educaition of children is a wide open field that needs entry from those competent to do this highly important work. The Valorian Society wants to move into this field but we recognize that any substantial change will require several generations to correct the harm done by the mass manipulators. At present attractive pictures are necessary to compete with the glossy materials the mass manipulators now buy with the enormous tax funds they obtain for "education." Because we do not have artists who want to draw competitive pictures, nor money to publish books of competitive glossiness, we are currently not giving this work the priority we think it merits. "Camp 38" contains a section that sets forth our current concept concerning sound education of children.

Removing children from the enemy-controlled schools that brainwash them for mass manipulation is the ultimate problem. The best of teachers become helpless if they must submit themselves to the existing system.

For the present, all sovereign individuals who are unable to educate their own children have the problem of finding some alternative to giving their children over to schools that brainwash them – whether the manipulators use words purportedly coming from a man-invented god, or the manipulative dogmas that they call "the consensus of scientific opinion."

The Valorian Society currently makes its major public appeal to perceptive adults. But neither we, nor any of the other sovereign individual groups that work outside the twisting influence of the mass media, have been able to make full use of all the opportunities. Some new ones are just now opening up.

The current facilities widely distributing video tapes for home viewing make it possible to use a new field of communication outside the censorship by the manipulators who control television broadcasts.

The rationally and emotionally improved lifestyle under the culture of individual sovereignty has never been set forth on the screen – either as a fictional possibility or as a historically accurate presentation. This shows that, despite each individual mass manipulator's greed for money, and the urgent need the whole industry has for new and different TV programs to satisfy the insatiable demand, the policy-making enemies of the United States are so fanatically committed to mass manipulation that they allow nothing favoring individual sovereignty to appear on TV broadcasts. Sovereign individuals, who have skills in the video field, now have an opportunity of unprecedented possibilities for clear, powerful communication.

There is hope for a glorious dawn in a near tomorrow if we of the Valorian Society, and others working in the same direction, can fully succeed in establishing effective communication between sovereign individuals.

SOVEREIGN PRESS

Dedicated to Individual Sovereignty

Sovereign Press proudly offers the following books by members of the Valorian Society.

The "American Christian Bible," extracted by Thomas Jefferson is included because it contains comprehensive comments by the Valorian Society member, Erik Holden.

The total body of the works here offered adds up to an organized attempt to communicate with those isolated individuals, and already established groups, who want to reclaim their innate individual sovereignty. These works present the results of extensive analysis, together with the Valorian Society's view of what actions can, and cannot, be effective in reaching a solution to the history-old human problem.

To indicate the scope of this carefully organized approach, we have included the Valorian Society's plan for discussion groups - divided according to the way the participants choose to approach the problem that now faces the human species.

SOVEREIGN PRESS, 326 Harris Rd., Rochester, WA 98579 U.S.A.

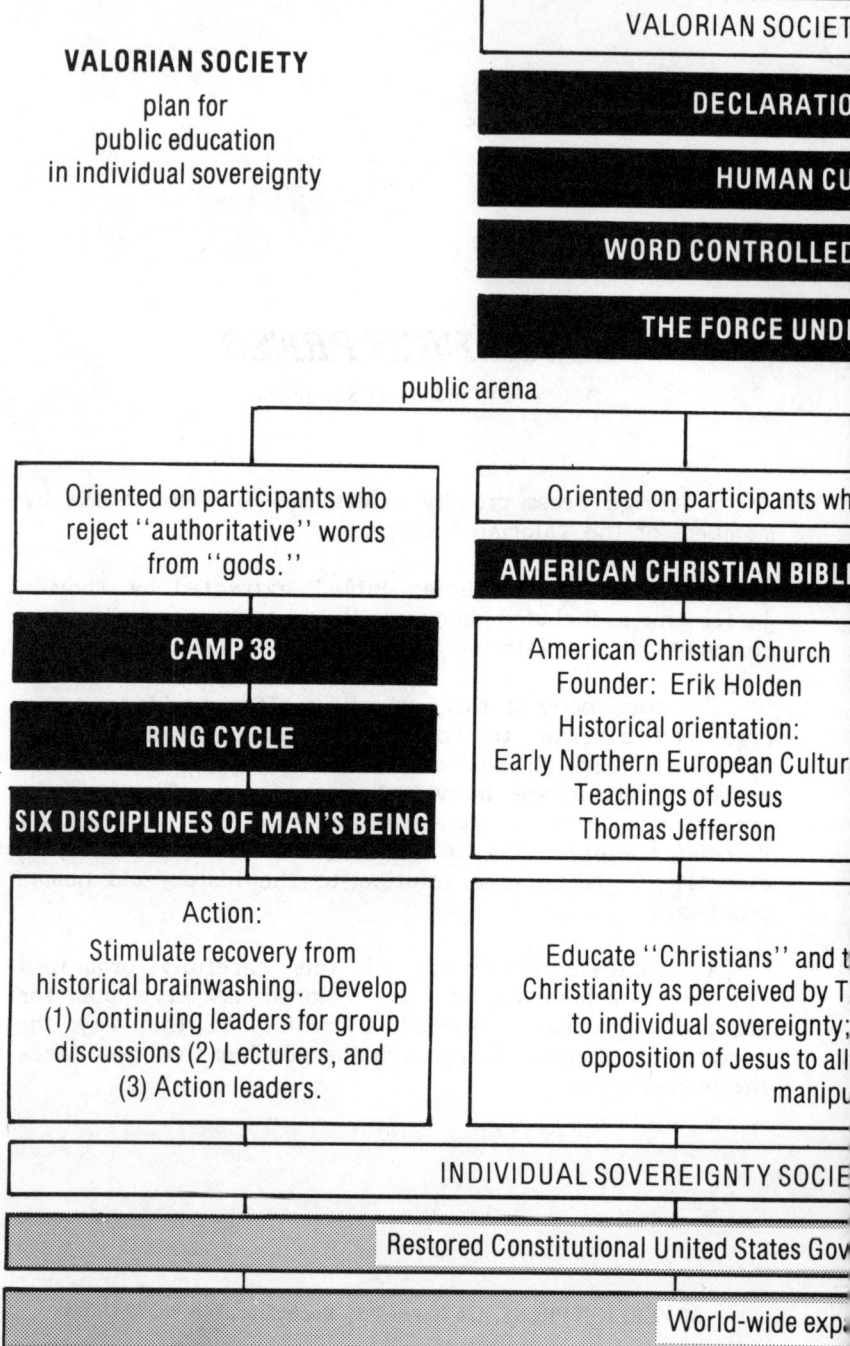

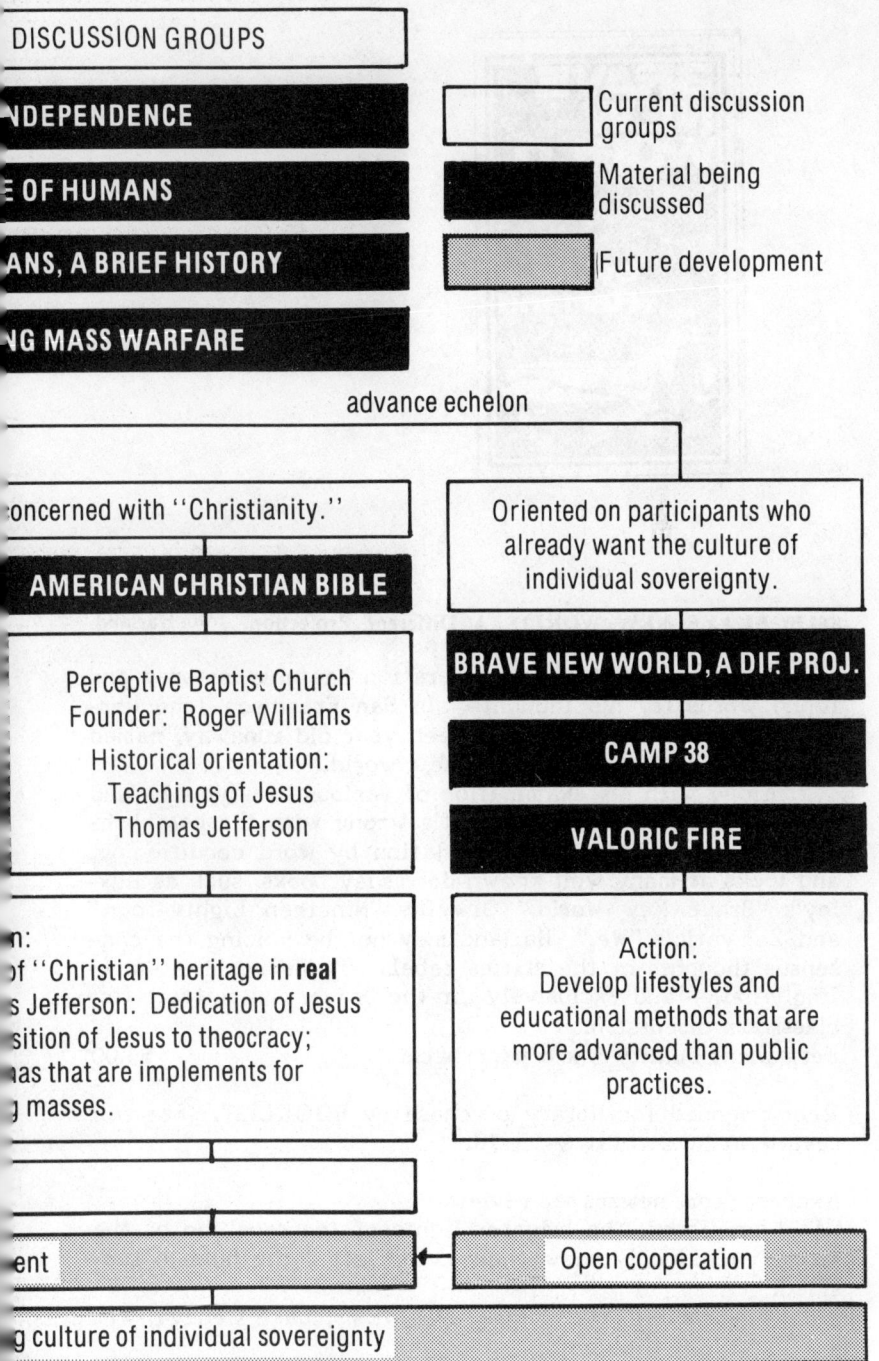

$5.00
paper
144 pages

84170 BRAVE NEW WORLD, A Different Projection. John Harland.

    A rebel of the sixties generation has now matured and found words for his thoughts. In San Francisco John Harland, at nineteen, and an eighteen year old runaway, named Jill, joined forces to create a new world.
    Along with his examination of various lifestyles he and Jill explored, he examines what's wrong with the establishment, with emphasis on manipulation by word conditioning, and looks at many well known doomsday books, such as Huxley's "Brave New World," Orwell's "Nineteen Eighty-four," and Zamyatin's "We." Harland may not be voicing the consensus thoughts of the sixties rebels but his world is startlingly new – and exclusively for the brave.   Suitable for classroom discussion.
Permanent quality 5 x 8 paperback $5.00

Recommended for library purchase by BOOKLIST. See full review in BOOKLIST 9-15-78.

Excerpt from newspaper review:
"As I predicted, the brighter lights of the rebellion of the sixties would only show their colors after the hubbub subsided."
        – Burton Frye, REGIONAL NEWS, Lake Geneva, Wis.

$6.00
paper
208 pages

84197 CAMP 38. Jill von Konen.

This is the Jill of John Harland's "Brave New World." After several years of living in a "full dress rehearsal for a culture of individual sovereignty," and discussing with everyone involved the possibility of having a real, fully effective culture in the present world, Jill presents a detailed, fictional picture of such a possibility. This projection of the most desirable life everyone participating in the "dress rehearsal" could imagine turned out to be what every fragment left of their history points to as being the actual practices and ideals of the early Northern Europeans. The "dress rehearsal" people then realized that what they were considering was not the usual, wild dream, pie-in-the-sky utopia. Their dream world was actually a current model of Northern European lifestyle before "Christianity." So, without making an issue of the distinction between real Christianity and what was promoted by the Catholic Church, Jill gave "Camp 38" a subtitle calling attention to this fact.

Her invented story covers the detailed day-to-day life under an imaginary full scale culture of the sort visualized by the secluded Valorian Society groups. Strangely enough, this yearned-for Camp 38, which now has to be only a dream, could have been a state, fully supporting and supported by the United States Constitution. If the Constitution were still functioning and some Federal land were made available, Camp 38 could be a realized dream even now. It is an extremely interesting idea on which to orient. Permanent quality 5 x 8 paperback $6.00

$5.00 paper
$9.00 hardcover
144 pages

79111 THE RING CYCLE. Melvin Gorham.

    This original work projects into the 21st century the age-old conflict of youths and lovers battling against the entrenched manipulators of public power. Hunding is portrayed as an official in the police-state of FAFNER, and the Valkyries are plane pilots who rescue wounded heroes from battle and take them to the individual sovereigns' haven in Valhalla. Brunnhilde, Chief of the Valkyries, challenges the authority of Wotan, the sovereigns' leader, when she attempts to aid Siegmund. The adaption to the 21st century setting makes an interesting background for Gorham's continuous story based on the plots of Wagner's "Die Walkure," "Siegfried," and "Gotterdammerung," all of which he follows closely. This will have special appeal for those interested in interpretations of the Ring operas. But none can fail to be caught up in the powerful dramatic material. This clear portrayal of the spirit permeating the Northern Europeans of prehistory opens the door on a whole new world where instinct and culture are in full agreement.

79111	Hardcover	$9.00
79103	Permanent quality 5 x 8 paperback	$5.00

    The first section, "The Valkyrie," had previous limited distribution in manuscript format for play production. This had a full review in LIBRARY JOURNAL 6-16-76 from which the following is quoted:

    "Recommended for university theater departments or those seeking a play with potential for experimental staging."

                                        – Susan F. Curtis, LIBRARY JOURNAL

$5.00
paper
128 pages

82146 AMERICAN CHRISTIAN BIBLE, extracted by Thomas Jefferson.

In 1904 Congress ordered the U. S. printing office to print 9,000 copies of the so-called Jefferson Bible for the use of Congress. These have largely disappeared and the work has been supressed. The reason for this is important to every American.

Jefferson, who wrote into the Declaration of Independence that governments derive their just powers from the governed, also wrote to Charles Thomson on January 9, 1816, "I am a real Christian." Seeking greatest Biblical accuracy, he compared Greek, Latin, French, and English versions and used scissors to cut away the theocratic injections that the 325 A. D. Council of Nice overlaid upon the teachings of Jesus. Theocratic Catholics and Jews have worked to suppress this Bible of a real Christian. Examination of Jefferson's views on Christianity draws attention to the fact that the Declaration of Independence, on which the United States was founded, clearly states rejection of theocracy.

This book contains a reproduced photocopy of Jefferson's work, along with an up-to-the-minute examination by Erik Holden of Christianity, biological development, and the all important relationship between religion, state, and individual sovereignty.

Permanent quality 5 x 8 paperback $5.00

$5.00
hardcover
296 pages

62012 THE PAGAN BIBLE. Melvin Gorham.

"Pagan" originally designated one who would not conform to the state religion of Rome. Later the word was used to point out – in attempted derision – one who would not conform to any of the currently popular religions around the Mediterranean: Official Roman "Christianity," Judaism, and Mohammedanism.

Accepting the challenge implied in the historical meaning of the word, Gorham examines all major religions of the world from the Pagan perspective. The examination sears more often than it praises but the end result is not a barren waste. From the seeming ruin, the ghost of a Pagan, who has endured generations of cloyingly benevolent group rule, rises up in heroic stature to demand a new incarnation.

The work arranges known realities into a conceptual framework that appeals to one who says "I am," "I perceive," and "I will." It shows that a fully conscious Pagan can find a way of life as far evolved beyond the institutional religions as the highest man is evolved beyond the most primitive organism of the Paleozoic slime. This is not a book for everyone, but the perceptive reader will arrive at a new plateau where a human individual has fully understandable meaning with relation to the total universe – and the total universe also has clear meaning.

Hardcover, 296 pages $5.00

$5.00
paper
128 pages

84189 VALORIC FIRE and A WORKING PLAN FOR INDIVIDUAL SOVEREIGNTY. From the Valorian Society.

This unusual book first sets forth an imaginary campfire conference of people with varied pasts who are seeking to form a totally new human relationship based on a new morality. It presents a view of individualism and the prospect for social cooperation as it might appear after passing through the fire of compulsory groupism.

Then it presents actual excerpts from the published – and quickly withdrawn from circulation – book by the "Old Man" who formed the alternative society described by John Harland's "Brave New World, A Different Projection." The excerpts include the exact wording for Agreements between Sovereign Individuals.

All who want to take part in any society or government seeking to be an alternative to the usual power structure of manipulated masses need to consider the ideas presented here. The facts and ideas here presented clarify the muddied ideological thoughts involved in most discussions of individualism versus "the greatest good for the greatest numbers."

Permanent quality paperback 5 x 8 $5.00

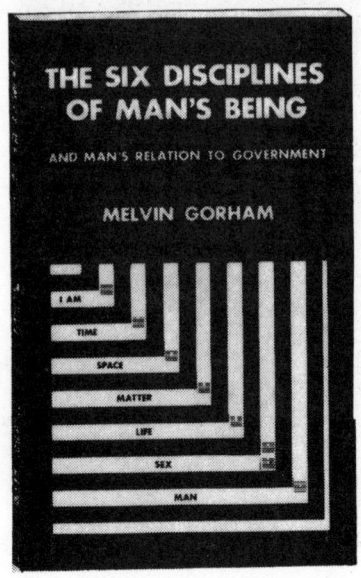

$5.00
paper
128 pages

83162 THE SIX DISCIPLINES OF MAN'S BEING and MAN'S RELATION TO GOVERNMENT. Melvin Gorham.

Gorham examines the life-direction pointed by evolutionary development and inherited memory, with special attention to the meaning of sex. He carefully defines (1) Time (2) Space (3) Matter (4) Life (5) Sex (6) Man, and posits "an ultimate frame of reference" for total reality.

After looking with new eyes at reality unencumbered by cultural trimmings, he considers governments. He sees most governments as surrogate parents that promote the anti-nature culture of mass manipulation. The history-old continuity of the oppressive practice suggests hopelessness. Then an opening is revealed which shows that a government can be the implement of all nature, and of nature's man, joined in one action. This is not a utopian dream of the future. It is a clear possibility and he presents a plan for immediate action.

Permanent quality 5 x 8 paperback $5.00

SOVEREIGN PRESS, 326 Harris Road, Rochester, WA   98579   U.S.A.

$5.00 paper
$9.00 hardcover
120 pages

81138 WORD CONTROLLED HUMANS, A Brief History. John Harland.

    Brief and crystal clear, this would be an admirable basic work before any other history is studied in the schools. The two major conflicting concepts of how life should be lived are described as cultural directions that came into conflict before that conflict reached a climax in the teachings and crucifixion of Jesus. The Holy Roman Church's use of a false Christianity to promote a theocracy is sharply portrayed as the destroyer of both the teachings of Jesus and the Northern European cultural direction.
    Then the American attempt to regain our cultural heritage of individual integrity is examined. The two hundred year long losing battle is covered from the perspective of religion, government, and money. Expanding to the worldwide scene, Harland looks at the errors made by the Germans under Hitler in trying to recover from the destructive effects of theocracy. He keeps his eye on what is significant rather than merely sensational.
    This brief history puts the problems of the human species into a context where effecive action to correct them can be seen as a present possibility.

81138   Hardcover $9.00
8112X   5 x 8 permanent quality paperback $5.00

SOVEREIGN PRESS, 326 Harris Road, Rochester, WA   98579   U.S.A.

83154 THE FORCE UNDERLYING MASS WARFARE.

This work sets forth the strategy of the Individual Sovereignty Society, ISS, for dealing with the causes behind the atomic bomb and all mass warfare – and for restoring Constitutional Government in the United States. Emphasis is on the unconstitutional power to control the value of U. S. money given to the Federal Reserve Bank, and the unconstitutional power of censorship given to those controlling radio and television broadcasting stations. Contains information about objectives, organization, and qualifications for membership in the ISS.
24 page brochure $1.00

84200 HUMAN CULTURE OF HUMANS, Valorian Society.

The focus is on the problem created by breeding for mass manipulation as it now exists in the United States – because the media is pushing our Government, despite our Constitution that opposes it, in the worldwide totalitarian direction. Bypassing the media that will not permit open discussion, this work presents a practical method for achieving its two immediate objectives: (1) Abolish the unconstitutional Federal Reserve System, and (2) Remove the unconstitutional "laws" that give the media power to censor open discussions and manipulate Congress. The necessary action to accomplish these objectives, which is already under way and rapidly accelerating, is precisely described.
32 page brochure $1.00

86235 HUMAN HISTORY 5 x 8 paperback, 112 pages $4.00
* * *
Sovereign Press gives booksellers the usual discounts and credit terms, has widespread sales through wholesalers who buy for libraries, the academic community, and the few retail stores that order special books for good customers. But we are not geared to the usual mass promotion of "best sellers." Because most bookstores are now so geared, you cannot usually find our books in retail stores. To meet this condition we maintain full mail order facilities.
Individual orders are welcome.

Publisher pays postage
(including foreign) when payment is included with order.
Take 40 percent discount on 10 or more copies same title.

SOVEREIGN PRESS, 326 Harris Road, Rochester, WA   98579   U.S.A.

ORDER FORM

To: **SOVEREIGN PRESS, 326 Harris Rd., Rochester, WA 98579 U.S.A.**

Publisher pays postage (including foreign) when payment in U. S. funds is enclosed with order. Take 40 percent discount on 10 or more copies of same title.

Quantity		Price	Extension
	American Christian Bible, Jefferson	5.00	
	Brave New World, Harland	5.00	
	Camp 38, von Konen	6.00	
	Force Underlying Mass Warfare	1.00	
	Human Culture of Humans	1.00	
	Human History, Valorian Society	4.00	
	Pagan Bible, Gorham hardcover	5.00	
	Ring Cycle, Gorham paper	5.00	
	Ring Cycle, Gorham hardcover	9.00	
	Six Disciplines, Gorham	5.00	
	Valoric Fire, Valorian Society	5.00	
	Word Controlled Humans, Harland p.	5.00	
	Word Controlled Humans hardcover	9.00	
	Sales Tax (Washington Residents)		
	Total (enclosed)		

Name _____

Address _____

_____ zip _____

ORDER FORM

Publisher pays postage
(including foreign) when payment is included with order.

Take 40 percent discount on 10 or more copies same title.

To:

SOVEREIGN PRESS, 326 Harris Rd., Rochester, WA 98579

Please send me the following: I enclose $ _____

Quantity	Title	Extension
	Sales tax (Washington residents)	
	Total	

Name _____

Address _____

_____zip _____